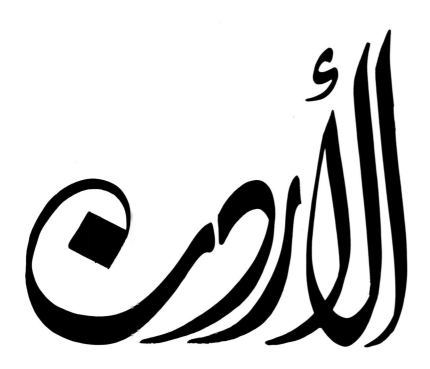

الأردن

بسم الله الرحمن الرحيم

Jordan
A Timeless Land

Christa Paula

David Saunders

Ammar Khammash

TransGlobe Publishing Limited
72 New Bond Street
London W1S 1RR
United Kingdom

books@tgmmc.com

First Published by
TransGlobe Publishing Limited 2005
© 2005 TransGlobe Publishing Limited

International Distribution by
I.B.Tauris & Co. Ltd.
6 Salem Road, London W2 4BU
United Kingdom

Text and captions copyright:
© 2005 Hossein Amirsadeghi
© 2005 Christa Paula

For full photographic credits and copyright
details see page 247

ISBN 0-9545083-2-7

A CIP catalogue for this book is available
from the British Library

Designed by Struktur Design
Reprographics by CS Graphics
Printed in Singapore by CS Graphics
Calligraphy by Yacoub Ibrahim

(Previous page) *Satellite image of the Southern Levant,
the Dead Sea and the Rift Valley*

Contents

Foreword

by Queen Rania Al Abdullah

صَاحبَةَ الجَلَالَة المَلكَة رَانْيا العبدُلله

Like the striated desert cliffs that mark the heart of this ancient country, today's Jordan is multi-textured, multi-hued and multi-layered. It is a land steeped in history, enriched with cultural treasures and inhabited by gracious people of diverse origins – many with roots in this land that go back centuries, others from Palestine, the Gulf States or beyond. At the same time, today's Jordan is a young, dynamic, forward-looking nation, a nation whose dreams for the future are as bold as the wonders of its past.

Aerial photographs reveal a landscape of incredible diversity and splendour. Yet impressive as Jordan is from this viewpoint, it is even more spectacular up close. It is walking through the serene valleys and rocky canyons of Wadi Rum, marvelling at the magnificent ancient architecture of Petra, visiting Moses' burial site on Mount Nebo or bathing in the mineral-laden waters of the Dead Sea, that Jordan's unspoilt natural beauty becomes clear. And it is meeting Jordan's people, sharing a meal or a stroll or a smile, that one appreciates how, through the ages, diverse communities have come together in this place and made it home.

Jordan's land has witnessed humanity's journeys throughout the ages. Many centuries ago, Hajj pilgrims travelled along the King's Highway. In biblical times, Christian pilgrims used our valleys and roads to reach sites venerated in their sacred traditions. In the 8th century, Umayyad caliphs and princes built stunning castles in Jordan's deserts. Later, crusaders built fortresses of their own at Karak and Shobak. And throughout, colourful convoys of merchants, their camels laden with silks and spices, enjoyed the serenity of the desertscape as they journeyed from Mecca to Bilad Esham.

To this day, Jordan remains at the crossroads of history. Thanks to the efforts of His Late Majesty King Hussein and my husband, King Abdullah II, Jordan has matured into a voice of mediation and moderation in the search for Middle East peace. We are also establishing ourselves as a model of economic and commercial reform in our region overcoming challenges and revitalising infrastructures to ensure our people are equipped to embrace the promise of the global age.

My husband and I believe that we are speaking for all Jordanians when we express our aspirations and our vision for Jordan. Jordanians share the common dream of building their country into a tower of strength, a refuge of peace, and a positive role model for the region. We know that Jordan is the place where Islam and democracy will co-exist comfortably and where tradition and modernisation will complement each other rather than compete acrimoniously.

It is this unique blend of pride in the past and hope for the future that characterises the modern Jordanian. I marvel at the fact that, in one short drive around Amman, I can see a Bedouin shepherd dreamily tending his flocks in a scene reminiscent of the Biblical era – and then, moments later, spot a tailored young executive making international business deals on her cell phone. Or, just as likely, the Bedouin shepherd will be chatting away on his mobile. Even more special, is the fact that these lifestyles co-exist comfortably and with mutual respect.

Grounded by and proud of such a colourful heritage, and strengthened by their unshakeable faith, the youth of Jordan, like

their forebears, possess impressive vision and drive.

In my meetings and conversations with young people around the country, I am constantly awed by their talent and dynamism. Equipping them with the tools to realise their dreams is one of our country's main priorities. With three quarters of our population under the age of thirty, the run-up to 2020 presents us, and our region, with an enviable demographic advantage. As birth rates decline and the age of the working population increases, we will have the highest ratio of potential workers to dependents of any region in the world. If we can harness this "demographic gift," we can achieve an amazing turn-around in our level of prosperity.

It won't be easy. But our young people are Jordan's future, and we want them to see a bright future in Jordan for themselves – to believe they can design and fulfil their ambitions proudly on Jordan's terrain. We are confident that by working together, we will create our own inherently Jordanian model for development, prosperity, and progress. It will be a model that embraces modernity and innovation, that speaks the language of the 21st century, that engages in the inter-religious dialogue and that interacts positively with other nations. Our success will contribute to the stability and promise not only of our country but our religion and the wider world.

His Majesty King Abdullah and I know that strengthening education, nurturing partnerships and encouraging investment are the best ways to create the hopeful future we seek. Only time will tell if we have got it right – but I truly believe that we are well on the way.

Of course, redesigning anything is a painstaking process and not without its difficulties. As the architects of change, we must respect what has gone before and be careful to preserve good practice, whilst also having confidence to experiment with new ideas and, if necessary, even break the mould.

But all of this has to be seen in the context of political stability in the region. Without peace and tolerance, building a foundation for our youth is a shaky business. Situated as we are on The Great Rift Valley, we know, as did the residents of Petra and Jerash, Madaba and Umm ar Rasas, the cost of investing time, effort and valuable structures on a land prone to major seismic activity. Just as the architect must take into consideration geological realities, so too must we build our future on flexible pillars. His Late Majesty King Hussein dedicated his life to securing a peaceful solution to the region's troubles. Both my husband and I are determined to uphold his noble work.

Confident in our place, comfortable in our heritage, Jordan can and will continue to be a connecting link between different nations, faiths and cultures to unite all people of good will. Ours will forever be a nation that believes in building bridges instead of walls, and that cherishes diversity rather than fearing it.

Our challenges are daunting. But I am convinced we can deliver opportunity and peace to our people, even in the face of adversity. I have seen my fellow citizens' fortitude etched into the walls of stone canyons. Time and experience have taught me that those who succeed are those who seek out opportunities, instead of being blinded by obstacles. Who would have thought that, in the midst of a bleak and forbidding desertscape of sand and stone, the ancient inhabitants of our land would envision and carve the soul-stirring city of Petra?

Our ancestors left us a legacy. They showed us that anything is possible if only we have the courage to raise our sights and the confidence to act. I believe that this is the spirit enshrined in the heart of every Jordanian today. And it is this spirit that will ensure we succeed on our journey to bring Jordan and the region greater prosperity, increasing opportunity and blessed peace.

Introduction

by Hossein Amirsadeghi

حسين أميرصادقى

"If anyone, no matter who, were given the opportunity of choosing from amongst all the nations in the world the set of beliefs which he thought best, he would inevitably – after careful consideration of their relative merits – choose that of his own country." Herodotus

Having travelled far and wide, I have encountered many cultures and beliefs in my time. Most have common threads binding our small planet's different civilisations; some are splendid in their isolation and others stand out for their special achievements in culture and history. Jordan, though small in land mass and poor in natural resources, is one of those nations. In one form or another, it has maintained greater continuity in historical purpose and more splendour in cultural attainments than many a larger state, existing or long disappeared, has achieved.

The Jordan River has been flowing through the veins of the world's three great religions: Judaism, Christianity and Islam since the age of Abraham. By extension, the religious cultures that underpin social and political history benchmark the events that have shaped present day Jordan. Moses viewed the Promised Land and died on Mount Nebo. Jesus was baptised at Bethany Beyond the Jordan. The Prophet Mohammed travelled along the King's Highway to trade as a merchant and alighted to heaven from Jerusalem's Temple Mount.

These great prophets performed many earthly duties on historical Jordanian soil. Mammon too, has been busy along these ancient imperial trade routes and military trunk roads. Egyptians, Persians, Greeks, Romans, Byzantines, Umayyads, Mamlukes, Turks and the British have all come and gone, have left their mark, and have been marked by the confluence of thought and religion embodied by this present day land of 93,000 square kilometres.

The Hashemite Kingdom of Jordan is a young country, but the land it occupies is an ancient one. Created out of the political and strategic chaos in the aftermath of the collapse of the Ottoman Empire at the end of World War I by Winston Churchill "with a stroke of a pen one Sunday afternoon," Jordan can rightly claim to be one of the more successful state-building exercises in imperial penmanship within its volatile neighbourhood. For most of its history, Jordan was part of a large and somewhat undefined region generally referred to as Greater Syria (not to be confused with present day Syria), a land mass encompassing the western part of the Near East bounded by Mesopotamia, the Mediterranean and Egypt. Scholars attribute the name to the Greek geographic description *Assyria*, derived from either the Semitic *Suriyon* or the Babylonian *Suri*. The Arabs called it *Ash Shams* or *Bilad Ash-Shams*, which simply means the North or the country of the north, as the Yemen was known as *Al-Yamam* – the South. This was the region between the Taurus Mountains and Sinai, between the desert and the sea, an area which the Hashemite dynasty of Mecca hoped to amalgamate into the Arab Kingdom of Syria, an imperial promise made (and not kept) by the British to the Sharif of Mecca, Al-Hussein bin Ali, in seeking his support for the overthrow of the Ottomans in 1916.

The Sharifs of Mecca were direct descendants of the Prophet Mohammed through his daughter Fatima and her husband Ali bin Abu Talib, the Prophet's paternal first cousin and the fourth caliph of

The King's Highway threads across Wadi Mujib, which, in biblical times formed the natural border between the Ammonites to the north and the Moabites to the south.

Islam. Ali had two sons, Al-Hassan and Al-Hussein. The direct descendants of the eldest son, Hassan, are known as *Sharifs'* (nobles), while the descendants of Hussein are called *Sayyids'* (lords). The present day royal family of Jordan is descended from the Sharfian lineage and the late King Hussein's branch of the Hashemite family ruled the holy city of Mecca from 1201 until 1925, recognising the sovereignty of the Ottomans from their conquest in 1517 until 1916.

From the beginning of time, Jordan's importance lay in its unique location as a nexus between some of the world's greatest civilisations, linking Egypt to Mesopotamia, Persia to the Mediterranean, the tribesmen of Arabia to the land of the Bible. Its inhabitants have through time knelt before pagan idols; Greek and Roman deities; and the One God in Jewish synagogues, Christian churches and Islamic mosques. It is a land of extraordinary contrasts and striking beauty; of rainbow coloured rocks, black basalt deserts and fantastical landscapes hewn out of time by geological rifts, dotted with painted castles in desert sands. This unyielding and surprising environment has tempered its people, both resolute and generous.

A finibus Syriae usque as Mare Rubrum (from the boundaries of Syria as far as the Red Sea) read the legends on some of the Roman milestones along one of the world's oldest trade routes, the King's Highway, denoting a distance of some 400 kilometres north to south from Bostra to Aqaba. This royal road on which merchants, soldiers, pilgrims and mendicants once travelled runs through history and through Jordan, connecting village to village, town to town, great cities to fabled lost civilisations. In biblical times it linked ancient Bashan, Gilead and Ammon in the north with Moab, Edom, Paran and Midian in the south. Today, it meanders across highlands and lowlands like the river of time that it is: the same road to which Moses was denied access on the Exodus, of which Herodotus wrote in the fifth century BC, the very same *Via Nova Traiana* of the Romans. Petra, the Red Rose City of history and fable, was one of the western termini of the great trading arteries of ancient times linking the King's Highway, the Frankincense Road, the Persian Royal Road and the Silk Road. Chinese annals refer to Petra as *Li-kan*, and from there, merchants would sort goods from China, India, south-east Asia and Africa for trans-shipment to Europe, through Mediterranean Sea ports like Gaza.

Roughly the size of Portugal, the Hashemite Kingdom of Jordan shares its borders to the west with Israel, to the north with Syria, to the north-east with Iraq and to the south-east with Saudi Arabia. Extending from the Gulf of Aqaba (Jordan's only sea port) in the south to the confluence of the Yarmuk and Jordan Rivers in the north, the country could not have been placed in a more unsettled political neighbourhood.

Topographically, it can be divided into three distinct regions: the rift, the highlands and the desert. The Rift Valley (part of the Great African-Syrian Rift) includes the Jordan Valley, the Dead Sea (both of which lie below sea level) and Wadi Araba. The earliest human settlers in the fertile Jordan Valley followed the route of the Rift from Africa into the Near East. The Dead Sea, the lowest point on earth, started as a series of fresh water lakes, and has shrunk over time to contain the highest salt-water concentration on earth.

The Nabateans, builders of Petra, were the Middle East's first oil merchants as they traded bitumen harvested from the Dead Sea to Egypt for embalming mummies, and to seafarers for caulking ships and boats. From its southern shores, the Rift becomes a hot and arid desert known as Wadi Araba, the "wilderness" of the Bible, rising 300 meters above sea level at its highest point, before it starts its slow descent towards the Gulf of Aqaba.

The highlands originated in the same tectonic plate movements that created the Great Rift Valley in Africa, with secondary rifts and ravines that made for natural borders between ancient kingdoms, and today afford spectacular sceneries enchanting tourists and travellers from afar. These highlands are divided into three main regions by major wadis. Between the Yarmuk and the Zarqa Rivers, the biblical Jabbok, lie the fertile growing regions; the centre around Amman is bounded by the Wadi Mujib, known in the Old Testament as the Arnon, and the south where the mountains rise higher and the lands become drier, is defined by the deep gorges of the Wadi Hasa, the Zered Valley of Deuteronomy.

Jordan is three-quarters desert, with only one major oasis (Al-Azraq meaning "The Blue" in Arabic) as the principal pivot for caravan routes from time immemorial. This divide between the desert and fertile lands has shaped the political history of Jordan, as nomadic Bedouin pastoralists have encroached on the settled fertile areas time and again, a source of conflict throughout its recorded history.

For travellers coming north out of the Arabian Desert, Jordan was the *masharif al-Sham* or "the approaches of Syria." And for those journeying south it was *masharif al-Hijaz* or "the approaches of the Hijaz." These routes carried pilgrims to the holy sites of Mecca and Medina via the Darb al-Hajj, a 40-day journey from Damascus to the Hijaz in earlier times. Even today, the oasis town of Ma'an serves as a major Hajj collection point though buses, not camels, form caravans to transport the faithful to the Holy Cities.

Modern Jordan mirrors this confluence of cultures and peoples with Circassians, Caucasians, Arabians and Palestinians all melding in a rich multicultural brew that is at once a rich source of social and economic ferment, and the cause of potential political instability. Of Jordan's population of 5 million over 95% are Sunni Moslems and 65% are of Palestinian origin. 80% of Jordanians live in around the urban sprawls

Jordan's economy has traditionally been based on agriculture and animal husbandry, with only 5% of the land arable. The principal crops are vegetables, wheat and citrus fruits with olives grown for the oil. Manufacturing is limited to such items as clothing, cement, foodstuffs and some oil refining, although pockets of industry are rising in strategic locations to support modernisation efforts lead by

The sixth milestone from Livias (far left), an ancient town identified with Tell Rama, was often mentioned by early Christian pilgrims who used it as a road marker for the holy site of Mount Nebo, where it is now displayed.

King Abdullah II (left) is today spearheading political and economic reforms at home and within the Arab World.

Petra, the cosmopolitan capital of the Nabataeans (right), was brought once more to global attention by the exploits of the Hollywood film character Indiana Jones.

the energetic young monarch, King Abdullah II.

Today, the country can boast one of the highest educated citizenry of any Arab nation, and the coterie of young Western-educated ministers and advisors around the King are pushing the theme of an information-technology and knowledge-based society, hoping to lay the groundwork for modern technology in a land that lacks natural resources. The country's balance of payments is heavily in the red, especially with regard to the import of oil and fuel, which Jordan relies on entirely from its rich neighbours.

The Jordanian leadership has to follow a fine balancing act both internally and externally, given the crosswinds of troubled Middle Eastern politics. The country's dependence on foreign oil and aid, its strategic and military reliance on America, its troubled but correct relations with Israel, Iraq and Syria all represent choices and dilemmas, one as difficult as the next. The late King Hussein had mastered this balancing act well, yet fell foul of his natural allies in 1991 when he sided with Saddam Hussein during the first Gulf War, paying a heavy economic and political price in the process.

His eldest son Abdullah, who assumed the throne on King Hussein's death in 1999, is today the most powerful figure in the country and it is he who appoints the cabinet and prime minister. There is a bicameral parliament, which has its origins in the first Organic Law instituted by the founder of modern Jordan, King Abdullah I in 1928, but the country only became independent of the British colonial yoke in 1946. Since 1974, both King Hussein and his successor King Abdullah II, have convened and dissolved parliament several times

King Abdullah II is today spearheading political and economic reform within the Arab world, in his attempts to bring good governance and public accountability to Jordan. Constantly on the move as a regional ambassador of goodwill, the monarch's open style of engagement with his people and their common shared problems comes across as a light touch compared to the political status quo in the region. Nevertheless, Jordan faces major problems that do not readily lend themselves to easy solutions based on Western models.

My own engagement with the country began nearly 30 years ago, upon first meeting the late King Hussein. I visited with him several times during this period, and became interested in Jordan as a subject for a book nearly a decade ago. It took a chance visit to Amman last year and a meeting with Queen Rania Al-Abdullah, for me to determine to finish the thought.

My aim in producing *Jordan: A Timeless Land* has been historically and pictorially inclusive with a comprehensive sweep through time and interrelated histories. But most importantly, I wanted to delight the reader with a vision of the country that is at once common and unique, spread across page after page of glorious photography: of Jordanian peoples, places and landscapes. In effect, I wanted to dazzle, as I had been dazzled myself. The success of the book is a tribute to my team, and to those Jordanians whose vision extends beyond the realms of bureaucracy.

Hossein Amirsadeghi
London, March 2005

The Prehistoric Era

Human activity in Jordan, as elsewhere, began over more than one and a half million years ago, at a time when sheets of ice blanketed one third of the planet's surface and the lower latitudes were blessed with rainfall. Small bands of hunter-gatherers followed migratory animals across the fertile steppes of today's desert belt that reaches from the Sahara, across the Middle East into the heartland of Asia. A chain of deep lakes filled the Jordan valley, and the Azraq and al-Jafr basins were covered by huge, shallow expanses of water teeming with wild life.

Earliest human settlements date back to the Lower Palaeolithic period, a good three-quarter of a million years ago. Prehistoric remains have been found in the Abu Habil formation in the Jordan valley, further north at Ubeidiyeh and Tabaqat Fahl, while the campsites littered with animal bones and stone tools around Azraq and in the highlands of Karak might even date earlier. There is also evidence for an Early Acheulian flaked stone industry 125,000 years ago. Certainly, by the Middle Palaeolithic period (100,000 – 40,000 BC) our human ancestors had spread throughout most areas of Jordan.

Although research into our earliest history is still in its infancy, we can assume that the southern Levant functioned as the only corridor for successive waves of human migrations from Africa. Around 40,000 years ago, modern man was established throughout the Middle East. In Jordan, the archaeological site of Wadi Hammeh suggests the presence of nomadic hunter-gatherers about 30,000 years ago. They were able to produce fine flint blades, possessed little and liked to meet up from time to time at designated localities.

The Azraq basin was a favourite environment for our ancestors. Radiocarbon dating places human occupation there to a quarter of a million years ago, and it remained there as the climate slowly became warmer. By the time of the late Mesolithic period (17,000 – 8500 BC) Azraq was a known gathering place. Occupation debris which spreads over an area of two hectares, prefigured the role the oasis was to play until the present. 'Azraq: the Blue' was a welcome relief from the desert, a nexus along trade routes, and a locus to celebrate life and to bury the dead. First evidence for long-range trade comes from this time, in the form of shells brought from the Mediterranean coast.

With the recession of the ice between 15,000 and 10,000 years ago, rivers and lakes started to shrink or disappear and large mammals were replaced by smaller, faster ones, like gazelles and wild goats. This environmental impact can surely be described as the single most important event in human history. New hunting techniques were required and invented, while an increased dependence on the gathering of grains fostered the development of new sophisticated tools.

The desert spread rapidly and resulted in what has been coined the Fertile Crescent: a green belt hugging the Great Arabian Desert in a broad arc, from southern Jordan up the Rift valley, from the Bekaa valley and the Lebanese and Syrian coastal plains to the Orontes, bending southwards to follow the Tigris and Euphrates rivers all the way to the Gulf. Similar environmental processes occurred along the Nile, the Indus and the Yellow River in China.

Along these rivers, early semi-permanent settlements began to develop, paving the way for the Neolithic Revolution. It was a period

Protected by a maze of sand-stone rock formations, al-Beidha (far left) is one of the oldest excavated Neolithic villages in Jordan. Six successive levels dating between 7200 and 6500 BC have been excavated, revealing semi-subterranean round houses and rectangular buildings, workshops and sacred places. Along with other sites on both sides of the Jordan River, al-Beidha was abandoned in the mid-7th millennium BC, never to be re-occupied.

Querns and grinders still lie scattered about the Neolithic site (left) of al-Beidha, where its ancient inhabitants produced surplus flour from wheat and wild barley for trade with nomads from the desert.

Located in the arid basalt desert of the windswept Hauran district near the modern border with Syria, Jawa (right) is one of the largest and best preserved Calcolithic cities anywhere. Upper and lower towns were constructed from volcanic rock, surrounded by massive fortifications and pierced by a large number of gates. Remnants of a citadel reign over the enigmatic site, while a highly advanced system of dams, reservoirs and canals were utilised to harness winter rains. Little is known of these masters of hydrology and why they chose such an inhospitable and isolated environment to build their stronghold 6000 years ago.

of major economic development. Complex settlements appeared in the Jordan valley, animals and plants were domesticated. The cultivation of wheat, barley and lentils along with the rearing of goats and sheep, later on of cattle and pigs, afforded a controlled food supply. Jericho, one of the oldest cities in the world, just west of the Jordan River was a leading centre for this development. To the east, it was followed by al-Beidha near Petra, where a local population had settled in the heart of a naturally fortified city producing surplus grain and flour for trade.

Around 6500 BC, another very abrupt change in climate, brought on by the melting of the continental ice-sheets in the northern hemisphere, caused decades of dry conditions in the Middle East. A 200 – year long drought forced people to abandon many sites – al-Beidha is one example – and to huddle near available water sources, thus setting the stage for rapid cultural evolution.

By the time Jericho was fortified 8000 years ago, a complex community had sprung up near modern day Amman. Ain Ghazal developed near a fresh-water spring still used today by pastoralists to water their animals, and is thought to be the largest archaeological site dating to the Neolithic period in the Middle East today. The village covered an area of 14 hectares supporting a population of

2000. Its inhabitants lived in small houses decorated with fine plaster and paintings, and built some of the earliest known temples in the world. They formed animals from clay for use in magic rituals and large human figurines from plaster to worship. Numerous ancient plaster statues have come to light, among them some extraordinary two headed busts, whose meaning can only be guessed. The eyes were always large and expressive and often inlaid with shells and bitumen to intensify the focus, an attribute that continued in the Middle Eastern artistic vocabulary until the iconoclast period in Islamic times. Bitumen, asphalt that floated in clumps to the surface of the Dead Sea, was first harvested during the Neolithic period, both for domestic use and for export. Luxury items were imported; shells and turquoise, basalt from the Hauran and obsidian from Anatolia, pointing to active interregional trade. There is evidence of sophisticated town planning, water conservation and of specialisation. Deceased family members were kept close by and usually buried beneath the living-room floor. Pottery made its appearance around 5500 BC, at a time when the village was already in decline.

By around 6000 BC, farming communities, both in the highlands and the Jordan valley, began to produce pottery of a style that has been termed Yarmukian. It is not known if this was a local

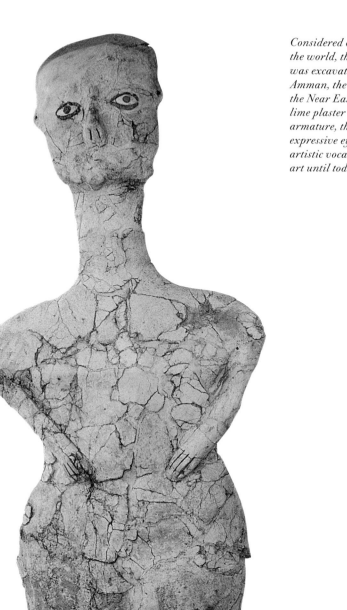

development or introduced from the north. We do know, however, that the climate had settled to become not unlike that of today, and that agriculture reached higher levels of productivity during the 5th millennium BC when it became, along with pastoralism, the main source of subsistence.

Scholars have long marvelled at the fact that while urban centres west of the Jordan such as Jericho were heavily fortified, settlements of similar magnitude flourished seemingly without defensive measures in the east. Early settlements like Pella, Abu Hamid, Sahab and Teleilat Ghassul come to mind. The large amount of metal weaponry, axes and arrow heads found at these sites, may have, at least in part, accounted for this elevated sense of security.

Sometime in the 5th millennium BC the art of copper smelting was discovered, bringing an end to the Stone Age and the beginning of the Calcolithic period (4,500 – 3300 BC). Malachite was gathered from deposits in Wadi Feinan south-east of the Dead Sea and shipped to smelting sites such as that of Abu Matar in the Negev. The copper objects found at Teleilat Ghassul exemplify true technological innovation, both, where they were poured in casts and when formed with the help of lost wax techniques. Currently, the assumption that copper working had its origins in Iran or Anatolia is

Dana Nature Reserve just off the King's Highway between the Crusader towns of Tafila and Shobak. The traditional village has been restored by the Royal Society for the Conservation of Nature and affords a spectacular view of the countryside and its diverse wild life. A track connects it with the ancient copper mines of Wadi Feinan.

'Azraq: the Blue' (right) *then and now a welcome relief from the desert.*

Ghassul presents a picture of a thriving community with highly developed aesthetic sensibilities. Many of its dwellings had been expertly decorated; walls were covered with fine plaster and painted in shades of red, black and yellow, with some blue and green in both geometric and naturalistic designs. A fragment displayed in the Citadel Museum, Amman, depicts three masked human figures in procession approaching what appear to be a group of buildings, a temple perhaps. There are horned masks and the ubiquitous exaggerated eyes, while a large eight-pointed star has been interpreted as a representation of the night sky. Imports tell of the ever increasing importance of trade, and of the wealth needed to purchase them. Syrian Tell Halaf ware, elegantly decorated with dark-brown slip, is found distributed from East Anatolia to Jordan, from northern Syria to Mesopotamia.

Perhaps as a reaction to the expansion of overland trade routes, a number of large towns prospered in peripheral areas between the "desert and the sown". Like many villages and towns in Jordan, Sahab due east of Amman on the way to Azraq, has been continuously inhabited since the early Neolithic Period. Now it was expanding and became dependent on resources imported from other areas around Jordan. Another much more enigmatic site is Jawa, located in the windswept semi-arid basalt desert of the Hauran, not far from the modern border with Syria.

Constructed of black volcanic rock, Jawa was intensely settled in the 4th millennium BC. It exhibits massive fortifications, thick inner and outer walls protecting packed domestic quarters, and a distinct citadel complex. Most of all, it is famed for its intricate water

being rethought by some archaeologists in favour of Jordan. Olives and dates were also introduced at this time, and as a more sophisticated population developed, burial customs changed with the advent of the graveyard, as did its relationship to the divine.

A number of astonishing wall paintings from Teleilat Ghassul illustrate an increasing concern about man and his place in the universe. First excavated by the Biblical Pontifical Institute between the two world wars and in 1977 by a team from Sydney University,

harvesting system. Over eight kilometres of canals, dams and reservoirs can still be made out. Annual winter rains and runoff water from the Wadi Rajil were ingeniously collected – a model well worth studying in a country notoriously lacking water. Who were the Jawaites and why did they settle in a region that even today is populated only by a handful of Bedouin families producing goat cheese for the Amman market?

Considering their advanced knowledge of water conservation, it has been suggested that they migrated from Mesopotamia. On the other hand, pottery fragments found in Tell Umm Hammad, a large settlement in the Jordan valley and the crossroads of two major trade routes, appear to be of the same type as shards found at Jawa, thus linking it to the Jordanian heartland. Geographically, it is situated between the fertile lands of the Damascene agricultural belt and the growing regions to the south-west, as well as near the trade routes from the east. Perhaps, most importantly, it is close to the desert inhabited by nomadic pastoralists who were also skilled hunters. Desert kites, huge traps constructed over vast areas to capture wild gazelles, ibex and oryx, have been found near Jawa, along with a number of petroglyphs depicting early hunting. Large scale gaming methods produced surplus meat, which could have been preserved and traded as a valuable commodity.

This socio-economic system is one familiar in Jordanian history, which has always juggled the desert and the settled lands with its geopolitical position as land-bridge between large centres of civilisation. Jawa itself had a relatively short lifespan. Within 50 years of its construction, it was utterly destroyed by unknown invaders.

Jordan – A Timeless Land

The Ancient Era

*T*he 5th millennium BC witnessed the rise of city states all over the Middle East. This phenomenon spread from southern Mesopotamia where civic centres, such as Uruk, were built around centralised temples which commanded agricultural hinterlands maintained by large-scale irrigation projects. Surplus production sustained an ever increasing population. Pictographs and the cuneiform script were developed to administer a diversifying labour force, which in turn fostered the evolution of social hierarchies. Wheeled vehicles facilitated transport, and trade became an integral part of local economies.

Similar processes occurred at Mari, Ebla, and in the Nile delta with the emergence of the Old Kingdom. Calendars regulated by the sun and the moon were invented, numbers introduced and monuments for god-kings soon rose against the desert sky. Byblos, on the Mediterranean coast, prospered as a result of its trade links with Egypt, supplying it with timber from the cedar forests of Mount Lebanon for the construction of the pyramids. Objects produced in Mesopotamia and Egypt, in Cyprus and Greece and found at archaeological sites throughout Jordan, suggest that the country's role as a trading nexus between the cradles of civilisations may well date back to this time, around the beginning of the Bronze Age (3200 – 1200 BC).

The early Bronze Age in Jordan is marked by an increased tendency towards urbanisation with significant changes in burial culture. Walled cities with watchtowers and bastions were being constructed, indicating a deep concern with security. Immigration to both sides of the Jordan River caused a rapid increase in population and, conse-

quently, resulted in new artistic trends. The painted pottery of the Calcolithic period was replaced by highly polished red-brown ware. A variety of new forms were introduced, and some vessels were being beautifully decorated with linear designs. Additionally, Levantine pottery has been found in Egyptian graves of the first Dynasty, while Egyptian imports were increasingly popular in Jordan.

A leading site for the early Bronze Age is the immense necropolis of Bab ad-Drah on the Lisan peninsula, which juts into the south-eastern waters of the Dead Sea. Near a fortified city, inhabited from 3250 BC until about 2350 BC, extends one of the largest graveyards of this period in the Near East. Some 20,000 graves have been counted thus far. The oldest equate with a number of shaft tombs, divided into chambers and filled with disarticulated bones. As is typical in secondary burial practice, skulls were kept separately, neatly arranged in a row to the left of the entrance, the grave goods to the right. Apparently, each chamber contained the remains of closely related families including infants and children. It is thought that these graves belonged to a nomadic people and that they predate the establishment of the city.

The second type of burial spans the lifetime of the adjacent town. Its citizens constructed large charnel houses, inclusive of doors and forecourt, where bones were deposited and stored without any discernible order. One such building contained the remains from over 200 people. When the city was abandoned, the necropolis continued to be used, although the earlier custom of shaft tomb burial was revived. Interestingly, pottery finds indicate that throughout its history, the site was primarily utilised by the

The vast mountain range near Petra presented a formidable barrier to early trade and exploration.

same people, recording first their transition to settlement and urbanisation and subsequently, their return to a nomadic or semi-nomadic lifestyle.

Following the abandonment of many of the early Bronze Age cities around 2350 BC, the entire region was thrown into a period of upheaval that lasted almost half a millennium. There have been attempts to connect this devastation to the cataclysmic destruction of the "five cities of the plain", Sodom, Gomorra, Admah, Zeboiim and Zoara (Genesis 19: 25). But while a number of likely candidates such as Bab ad-Drah, Numeira and Feifeh show signs of destruction by fire, most scholars date Abraham and Lot, who allegedly pastured his sheep along the eastern shores of the Dead Sea during this event, to around 1900 BC. More commonly, the rise of a west-Semitic tribe, the Amorites, is blamed for the demise of Early Bronze Age civilisation.

Known by the Egyptians as the Amu and by the Sumerians as the Maru, the Amorites appeared from the Syrio-Arabian desert, sweeping across Mesopotamia and into the Levant, where they became known as the Canaanites. From 1900 to 1600 BC, they administered a number of city-states centred around Babylon (hence, Old Babylonians), the temporal and spiritual capital of the famous Amorite ruler Hammurabi. This intermediate period also coincided with the breakdown and dissolution of the Old Kingdom in Egypt, and major upheavals in Mesopotamia, where the Sumerians were deposed by invaders from the Iranian plateau. During the same time, Abraham and his household entered from Mesopotamia. The Canaanites referred to them as the *haribu*, wanderers, from which the name Hebrew is derived.

Within a century of the reunification of Egypt under the Middle Kingdom (2052 BC) and the restoration of the Third Dynasty of Ur (2050 BC) a new epoch began for Jordan. Thus, it appears that the sudden urban collapse in late third millennium BC cannot be attributed to a single event but to a combination of factors. Overpopulation and disasters at home, the interruption of international trade with Egypt and Mesopotamia, and the pressure caused by the assimilation of several waves of newcomers, set a pattern repeated again and again throughout Jordan's long history. The local population simply adapted by returning to a nomadic or semi-nomadic life-style, creating smaller, more ephemeral settlements.

While recovery was slow, there was never a complete hiatus from sedentary life, as some earlier archaeologist have suggested. So far, some two dozen Middle Bronze Age (1900 – 1550 BC) settlements have been discovered along the east bank of the Jordan River alone. Grave goods from Pella, Irbid, Amman and Sahab, to name but a few, indicate a revival of trade and increased prosperity.

Meanwhile Egypt, under the Middle Kingdom, was entering its most glorious period. Trade routes were re-established and Egyptian influence reached far into the Southern Levant. For the first time, Jordan was mentioned in literary documents. Both the Egyptian Execration Texts (ca. 1880 – 1810 BC) and the Mari letters from central Syria (19th –18th century BC) reveal organised international trade in tin which, along with copper, is the main ingredients in the production of bronze.

From the earliest days, trade routes not only facilitated

commercial traffic but also functioned as avenues for the exchange of knowledge. Thus, new medical practices were being introduced into the region. A curious skull in the Citadel Museum, Amman, for example, exhibits evidence of trepanning, an ancient surgical practice that involved boring holes into patients' skulls. A number of prehistoric trepanned skulls have been found in dolmen burials in Algeria, leading to the conclusion that it was a common operation among proto-Berbers. In the 5th century BC, the "father of history" Herodotus of Halicarnassus, observed that the "Libyans" cauterised the heads of their children at the age of four, "*to prevent them from being plagued in their after-lives by a flow of rheum to the head.*" Intriguingly, the art of trepanning became a global phenomenon and continued to be practised in some parts of the world until the modern era.

For the remainder of the Middle Bronze Age Jordan, along with the rest of the Levant, fell under the influence of the Hyksos, a group of mixed Semitic-Asiatics who settled in northern Egypt sometime during the 18th century BC. In about 1630 BC, though earlier dates have been suggested, they overthrew the 14th Egyptian dynasty, which was already plagued by domestic political problems. The Egyptians called them the *hega-khase*, "rulers of foreign lands".

Josephus, the first century AD Jewish historian, translated it as "king-shepherds" and attempted to identify the Hyksos with the Hebrews. Other historians have seen proto-Edomites in them, the later inhabitants of the southern Jordanian Iron Age kingdom of Edom. Many of the Hyksos names are indeed Semitic, though some show Hurrian traces (co-founders of the 15th century BC Mitanni kingdom in northern Mesopotamia). In any event, the Hyksos brought with them knowledge of superior weaponry and military architecture, the horse-drawn chariot and Canaanite-style temples. They adopted the Egyptian storm and desert god Seth as their principal deity.

For Jordan, the Hyksos period once again brought a population explosion. Finds of rich grave goods denote a period of prosperity and perhaps a change of attitude towards the afterlife. One grave site at Pella yielded no less than 2000 small items, including scarab seals, trinkets and jewellery. Fine, thrown pottery, reslipped and burnished, is widely found, while the locally produced Hyksos period Chocolate-on-White-Ware was distributed throughout the Levant. At the same time drinking vessels and jugs in the shape of animal or human heads became popular, while abundant finds of gold jewellery speak of wealth and of amusement in its display.

This strongly stylised female figurine (far left) carrying an amphora was excavated from an Early Bronze Age shaft tomb in the extensive necropolis of Bab ad-Drah. Situated 250 metres below sea level on the Lisan peninsula on the south-eastern edge of the Dead Sea, this site is currently a favourite candidate for one of the biblical "Cities of the Plain".

Perhaps once used for ritual libations, this unique zoomorphic jug (left) was modelled by a local craftsman over four thousand years ago. There are no comparative examples of this vessel type, which beautifully incorporates the elements of earth, air, water and fire to create a meaningful and utilitarian object of art.

In 1550 BC, Amosis, the first Pharaoh of the 18th dynasty, expelled the Hyksos from the Nile delta, heralding the beginning of the New Kingdom (1570-715 BC) in Egypt and the Late Bronze Age (1550-1200 BC) in Jordan. He pursued them without mercy up the Levant littoral and into Syria until they dispersed into the north-eastern borderlands. Jericho, Megiddo, and possibly Sahab, south-east of Amman, were destroyed during this campaign.

The entire region was affected when Egypt took on the role of leading superpower. It was vigorously expansionist and, under Amosis' successors, extended its influence to the periphery of the Mesopotamian heartland. Thutmosis III (1468-1437), who based his administrative centre in Gaza, carried out no less than 16 military invasions into the Levant.

Possibly because of the safety gained from Egyptian hegemony, whose primary interest would have been to maintain the integrity of the trade routes, goods from all directions passed through Jordan. Materials excavated at the Old Amman airport, at Deir Alla and Tell Irbid, revealed items from Egypt, Cyprus, the Aegean, Syria and Mesopotamia, along with locally produced artefacts whose composite styles reflect influences from various artistic centres. Seals, in the form of scarabs, cylinders and stamps, used

throughout Middle East and Egypt since the fourth millennium BC, were imitated. Many of the destroyed settlements were rebuilt, bigger and better, exhibiting sophisticated city planning with well-organised water and canal systems. By the 15th century BC, Sahab was fortified and had become a flourishing centre on one of the main eastern access routes to Amman.

This flowering of Transjordanian culture is also substantiated by a large number of clay tablets found at Amarna, capital of the "Heretical Pharaoh", Amenophis IV, written in cuneiform characters and in the diplomatic language of the day, Akkadian. They reflect a lively exchange between the Egyptian administration and its representatives abroad, concerning the state of international affairs between Egypt and the major and minor powers of the Middle East. Of note is a letter (EA 244) by one Biridiya complaining about the uncooperative Labayu, who had his powerbase at Pella, an important staging point on the east-west route near a main ford across the Jordan River. Much of the correspondence, however, was concerned with the menacing presence of the Hittites, an ancient Indo-European people who had united and sacked Babylon in the mid-16th century BC, and were threatening to expand westward. In the northeast, Hurrians and Mitanni had moved into northern Mesopotamia and had consolidated into the Mitanni kingdom, which, in its heyday reached from the Zagros Mountains in Iran and Lake Van in Anatolia to Assur on the upper Tigris River.

For a time, the three powers formed a triangle, struggling for regional domination and squeezing Jordan and the Levant between them. Eventually, the Mitanni were absorbed by the Hittites, and a

Typical Chocolate-on-White-Ware from Middle to Late Bronze Age Pella, exhibited in the Archaeological Museum Irbid. Produced locally, this pottery type was widely distributed throughout the Levant during the Hyksos period.

The scarab has its roots in Egypt where it was called Cheper, "he who becomes", and was worn as an amulet representing the god of transformation. Later, the flat bottom surface was engraved with the symbol and name of the owner and used as a seal. The scarabs illustrated here come from Pella and are thought to date from the Hyksos period. The nude goddess flanked by palm trees remained a favourite motif in Transjordan throughout the Middle Bronze and Early Iron Age.

great battle ensued in southern Syria at Kadesh in 1299 BC between the two remaining opponents. Both sides claimed victory and a balance of power was restored, with the boundary to Egyptian controlled land being drawn along the Orontes River.

But times were changing. The use of bronze facilitated stronger weapons and better tools. Horses, oxen and donkeys were used both for transport and labour. At Ugarit in the 14th century BC, then in Byblos in the 13th, the alphabet triumphed over the cumbersome system of cuneiform writing. In the Syrio-Arabian Desert, in the steppes of Central Asia, the Iranian Plateau and around the Mediterranean, people were on the move. Weakened by repeated invasions from northern tribes, the empire of the Hittites fell apart. At the same time, the Aramaeans were advancing towards Syria where they eventually founded Damascus, while the "Sea People", a motley crew of pirates, merchants and mercenaries of diverse origins, caused or coincided with the collapse of trading centres around the Mediterranean. Finally, around 1250 BC, Moses gathered together the tribes of Israel and journeyed across the Sinai towards the Promised Land.

Owing to this precarious international climate, the old Transjordanian city states began to unite to form larger, territorially-based nations. Their names are familiar to us from the Old Testament – Edom, Moab, Ammon – while their geography extended south to north along the mountainous spine of Jordan's highlands, abutting its lifeline, the King's Highway.

The last segment of the Exodus story is played out against the backdrop of this new political map. Both, Edom and Moab famously refused access to the King's Highway to the Israelites, who, skirting these territories, vanquished the Amorite statelets of the Kings Sihon and Og. Moses died in Jordan after gazing upon the Promised Land from the heights of Mount Nebo, while Joshua led the people across the river. There, the Israelites established ties with existing tribes and formed the *Amphictyony*, or League of Twelve Tribes, a political union focused on a centrally located shrine, and led by "Judges". Gad, Ruben and half of the tribe of Manasseh were allocated conquered land on the East Bank. The following centuries were marked by deep enmity between these nominally related people from both sides of the river Jordan.

Despite heavy campaigning by Pharaoh Merneptan in 1220, the *Peleset*, a splinter-group of the Sea People originally from the Aegean and Anatolia, ousted the Egyptians from their stronghold at Gaza, and founded a number of city states along the coast. They became known as the Philistines, and eventually gave their name to the entire region. Knowledge of iron-working techniques explains their military superiority. By 1000 BC, these skills had spread throughout the region, ushering in the Iron Age (1200 – 539 BC)

The collapse of Egyptian hegemony over the Levant had left a power vacuum, facilitating the creation of a number of smaller kingdoms. The Phoenicians began building their Mediterranean trade monopoly, while the Israelite tribes settled and consolidated. At the same time, the southern Arabian incense producing regions underwent a similar process. By 1010 BC, Saul was proclaimed king, defeating the Philistines on the plains of Jezreel. His son, Ishbaal

This unique ivory box from the Late Bronze Age was found next to two Babylonian cuneiform tablets during excavations at Pella. Although the overall form exemplifies classical Egyptian design, incorporating djed *pillars as symbols of cosmic stability, other elements lean on Mesopotamian iconography. The winged sun disk is the emblem of the Assyrian god Asshur, while the heraldic lions flanking two intertwined snakes point to design conventions common throughout the Middle East. It is generally thought that the box was produced by a local craftsman, elegantly merging elements from a variety of traditions.*

ruled the north of the country. Under David (1006-966), Judaea and Israel were united and Jerusalem was established as its religious and political centre. It was a time of almost continuous battle, of borders being drawn and redrawn. David was succeeded by his son, the legendary King Solomon, and Jewish history entered what is now considered its Golden Age. In response, Edom, Moab and Ammon began to flex their muscles.

The Edomites inhabited an arid landscape. The deep canyon of Wadi Hasa – the Zered Valley of the Bible – provided a natural northern border; to the south they abutted the Red Sea. The Great Arabian Desert lay to the east, while Wadi Araba with the rich copper mines of Wadi Feinan defined Edom's territory in the west. In the Old Testament their ancestry is attributed to Essau, son of Isaac and Rebecca, who sold his birthright to his brother Jacob (Genesis 25: 30). Edom, land of bizarre sandstone formations, of the natural fortress of Petra and the pink sands of Wadi Rum, became the largest of the Transjordanian Iron Age kingdoms.

Located in close proximity to Egypt via the Sinai trade routes, the Edomites are often mentioned in early Egyptian inscriptions and, more prominently, in the Amarna letters. Indeed, Ramses II boasted about his frequent and always bloody military excursions against them. In the Old Testament they are referred to in connection with the Exodus saga, when they denied access to the King's Highway to the Israelites on their migration to the north (Numbers 29: 14-21). King David is recorded to have slaughtered a large part of Edom's male population (1 Kings 11: 5) and to have deployed military governors to subdue the region, while King Solomon is reputed to have exploited their copper mines in Wadi Feinan, exporting the precious raw material from the elusive harbour of Ezion-Geber somewhere in the region of modern Aqaba. In the ninth century BC, the kingdom was able to re-establish its independence, only to be invaded again in the eighth century.

The eighth century BC saw incursions by Tiglathpileser III (745-727 BC), megalomaniac and architect of the "Assyrian world-dominion", and tribute was extracted from Edom by him and his successors. By the late seventh century BC, the Assyrian Empire was disintegrating, and all of the trading kingdoms suffered greatly from Bedouin raids. Ammon, the central kingdom north of Edom and Moab, pleaded for help and found it in the builder of the tower of Babel, Nebukadnezar II (604-562 BC), second emperor of the New Babylonian Empire. As a result, Jerusalem and Rabbath-Ammon were destroyed, and mass deportations threatened the very existence of all the kingdoms.

In 1971 archaeologists matched the biblical Bozrah with Buseirah, a site located just off the King's Highway between Tafila and the Dana nature reserve. Despite being viciously cursed by both Isaiah (34: 5-17) and Jeremiah (43: 7-22), the Edomite capital flourished from the seventh century BC to the Persian period. It was solidly fortified and must have played a significant role on the budding trade routes from Arabia, attested to by a number of camel statuettes which are thought to be votive offerings from long-distance traders. Its main natural resources, however, were copper from Wadi Feinan and bitumen from the Dead Sea which were exchanged with commercial centres throughout the region.

Jabal Haroun and Aaron's tomb near Petra. According to the Old Testament, Moses was ordered by God to bring his elder brother Aaron to the top of Mount Hor. There, "Moses stripped Aaron of his garments, and put them upon Eleazar his son; and Aaron died there in the top of the mount." (Numbers 20). Jabal Haroun has long been the designated site for this particular Exodus story and was even venerated as a holy mountain by the Nabateans. Later, a Christian monastery was built there and continuously occupied until the 13th or 14th century. Aaron subsequently became an important prophet in the Islamic tradition.

Nominally a desert nation living by trade and raid, the Edomites had a special affinity with high places, strongholds hidden amongst inaccessible crags and canyons. There are a number of them in and around Petra, but the most enigmatic of them all, Sela, is located not far from the ancient Bozrah. Difficult to find, Sela is approached through a rock-cut access and reached by a steep staircase. Ingenious water harvesting features are visible everywhere, and a profusion of archaeological remains are spread across a flat high plateau. Surprisingly, there have been no excavations of note at Sela, whose name derives from the Hebrew word, "rock". Surface finds indicate that it served as a hiding place, a refuge, from the Bronze Age to the Mamluke period in the 14th and 15th centuries of the Christian era.

For some scholars, Sela is a likely candidate for the biblical "rock" connected with Amaziah of Judaea (796-767 BC), who brutally attacked the Edomites. He defeated them in a battle in the Valley of Salt and captured Sela (2 Kings 14: 7). Subsequently, he took 10,000 captives and *"brought them unto the top of the rock, and cast them down from the top of the rock, that they all were broken in pieces."* (2 Chronicles 25: 12). The other candidate as a likely source for this story is a similar lofty fortress, Umm al-Biyara in Petra.

Barely discernible with the naked eye halfway up the sheer cliff face to the left of the staircase, a large bas-relief depicting a Mesopotamian king accompanied by extensive cuneiform inscriptions has been carved into the Sela rock face. The crescent of the moon god Sin, the winged disc of Asshur, and the star of Ishtar, divine personification of Venus, are placed above the monarch. The king has been tentatively identified with the Babylonian ruler Nabonidus (555-539 BC), who not only blazed through Edom during his military expedition to Arabia, but also left a visible symbol of his presence on this obviously important and all but impenetrable natural fortress. Sela's proximity to the Edomite urban centre, its

This 10th century BC sarcophagus lid from Sahab (left) represents a type relatively common throughout Transjordan between the 12th and the 8th centuries BC. The Osiris beard decorating the sleeping face hints at Egyptian influences, while the execution already alludes to idiosyncratic Ammonite and Moabite sculptural styles.

The Mesha Stele (right) was discovered by the German missionary F.A. Klein in 1868 in Dhiban and eventually purchased piece by piece by Clermont-Ganneau. This large basalt stone embodies the only literary record outside the Old Testament for mid-ninth century BC Jordan. Written in a language closely related to an early form of Hebrew, the inscription is dedicated to the Moabite god Chemosh in thanks for the deliverance of King Mesha (ca. 853BC) and his subjects from the Israelites. Mesha has been identified with the biblical shepherd-king (2 Kings 3:4). At the time, Omri had occupied the Madaba region whence he was threatening Moabite positions. Originally inscribed with 35 lines, this extraordinary stele has preserved for posterity not only Mesha's military exploits, but also refers to his building projects and duties as a ruler. The original is now housed in the Louvre, Paris.

obvious attraction to later invaders and its extensive occupation by the Nabataeans during the following centuries, can only reinforce theories supporting its identification with the biblical "rock".

Not long after Nabonidus carved his edicts into the Sela rock, Cyrus II turned Babylonia into a Persian province (539 BC) and began his great expansion south. The Edomites had had enough. They gathered together their animals, packed up their belongings and slowly moved off to the region between the Sinai and Israel, a quiet land off the beaten track, later known in history as Iduemaea.

The territory of Moab extended from the northern border of Edom to the Wadi Mujib – the biblical Arnon River – and at times as far as the plains around Madaba. On the east-west axis, it incorporated the land between the desert and the Dead Sea. It bordered on Ammon, which occupied the land up to the Wadi Zarqa – the ancient Jabbok River – and had its capital at Rabbath-Ammon, Jordan's primary urban centre and great crossroads on the international trade routes.

The Old Testament traces the origins of both kingdoms to the incestuous relationship between Lot and his daughters: *"thus were both daughters of Lot with child by their father. And the first-born bare a son, and called his name Moab: the same is the father of the Moabites unto this day. And the younger, she also bare a son, and called his name Ben-ammi: the same is the father of the children of Ammon unto this day"* (Genesis 19: 37-38).

No doubt the Moabite state was built in reaction to the continuous military threat, although the advantage of a consolidated government in light of the ever-increasing flow of goods along the

King's Highway should not be underestimated. In alliance with Ammon, Moabite mercenaries crossed the Jordan River and laid siege to Jericho. King David retaliated and in turn took Moab and Ammon. He besieged the Ammonite capital, took the crown of their god Milkom, extracted one of its precious stones and incorporated it into his crown. (2 Samuel 12: 30). It was during this campaign that David fell in love with Bathsheba, wife of the Hittite Uria, marrying her after her husband died beneath the city walls of Rabbath-Ammon. Solomon was their offspring. During the reign of King Solomon, the Ammonites remained vassals of Israel. Solomon even took an Ammonite wife who gave birth to a later king of Judaea. After Solomon's death, Israel divided into two kingdoms, and control over Jordan weakened, only to be reasserted by King Omri of Samaria.

From this period of unrest, comes one of the most important primary literary source for the Iron Age history of Transjordan, the

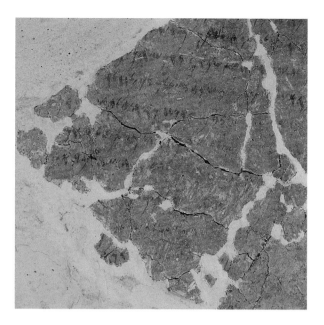

This seated monkey (left), *which appears to be supporting a lamp on his back, was buried in a grave at Tell Safut sometime during the Iron Age. The monkey is often connected with the Egyptian lunar deity Thoth, who was believed to replace Ra, the sun, while the latter made his nightly journey through the underworld.*

A few kilometres from Pella (right) *rises the impressive Tell Deir Alla. Often identified with the biblical Succoth, the site was inhabited from about 4000 BC until the invasions by Alexander the Great's generals. Later it was reused as an Islamic graveyard. During the 1967 excavations, fragments of a unique document executed in ink on plaster came to light. Written in a north-west Semitic dialect, it is by far the oldest known literary text in Aramaic. It was composed at the same time as the Book of Amos and includes a revelation by well-known prophet and professional curser Balaam, son of Beor. Balaam was beseeched by King Balak to help against the Israelite incursions into Moab (Numbers 22-24).* "And man will mock the wise", *he warns us in this long rant dated very liberally to 800 BC.*

Mesha Stele. This large basalt slab records a thanksgiving by the Moabite king of *Qarha* to his god Chemosh and records his battles against the Israelite King Omri, as well as his civil achievements. The location is possibly a village in the Karak region. The language is one of the few known examples of Moabite, which was related to the biblical Hebrew and Canaanite, languages spoken before they were replaced by Aramaic in the sixth century BC. Canaanite, Aramaic and Arabic belong to the same Semitic language family. The word Semitic is derived from Shem, son of Noah, who is named in the Bible as the common ancestor of the Hebrews, Aramaeans and Arabs

In the ninth century BC the New Assyrian Empire began to assert itself, culminating in the domination of Jordan by Tiglathpileser III (745-727 BC) and his successors. Like Edom, Ammon and Moab managed to retain some form of independence in exchange for tribute payments. In the service of Assyrian interest, the Moabite King Kamosh Haleth is even recorded to have repressed a Bedouin uprising in Wadi Rum.

Ammon's fortunes took a similar path, and a number of tribute-paying kings, Sanipu, Bod-el, and Aminadab are sited in Assyrian sources of the time. In 721 Sargon II, "Just Ruler" of Assyria, destroyed Samaria, inaugurating a period of uneasy peace and renewed prosperity.

Pottery found in graves from this time is finely produced and beautifully decorated. A new sculptural tradition was developed, incorporating stylistic influences from Assyria, Aramaic Syria and Egypt, and executed in a quintessentially local style. The Frankincense-producing regions of present-day Yemen had devel-

oped into powerful trading nations. Saba, the kingdom of the legendary Queen of Sheba, was experiencing its heyday, controlling the South Arabian caravans from the late eighth century BC for the next 200 years. Its wealth, gained from frankincense and myrrh, cinnamon, cassia and gold ultimately benefited the Levantine commercial centres and cities such as Amman, which was located on the cross-routes of international trade between the desert and the Mediterranean Sea.

After the fall of the Assyrians and their replacement by the short-lived Neo-Babylonian Empire, attacks by desert Bedouins increased. The Edomites moved west to leave a power vacuum that would eventually be filled by Arab nomads of the Qedar tribe, later known as the Nabataeans, while Ammon and Moab, along with the rest of the Levant were incorporated into the Persian Empire's 5th Satrapy. The Iron Age kingdoms of Transjordan ceased to exist as nominally autonomous states.

Following his conquest of the Medes, Cyrus the Great (559-529 BC), of the house of the Achaemenids, quickly consolidated his power over Persia. Equipped with superior battle techniques learned from the "barbarians" of the steppes, mounted warriors armed with bow and arrows commanded by the guard of the "Immortal Ten Thousand", swept across the Middle East towards Egypt. Military might was supported by an innovative administrative system, which divided the new empire into satrapies, whose primary task was to maintain standing armies and supply labour for public works. Aramaic was used as the language of government and business,

This remarkable sculpture (above) has been identified by inscription with Jerach-Azar, grandson of the well-known Ammonite king Sanipu. It was retrieved from the foot of the Roman wall of the Amman Citadel. Typical of 8th century BC Ammonite sculpture, it is a composite of stylistic influences. The left hand clasps a lotus flower, long the sign of kingship in Egypt, while the garments remind one of Aramaic dignitaries. The proportions favour the head and the focus is on the eyes, which were once inlaid.

This beautiful male head (top) with Osiris beard and thick curly hair was found in 1949 along with the sculpture of Jerach-Azar near the Amman Citadel.

Horse and Riders (above) with conical helmets from the 7th century BC sculpted from clay, excavated from an Iron Age grave in Maqablain near Amman.

7th to 6th century BC alabaster makeup palette (top) probably from the Amman Citadel. Similar toiletry articles have been found at the Edomite bastion of Umm al-Biyara above Petra.

5th century amphoriscos of blue and yellow glass (above) from Umm Udaina near Amman. This miniature replica of a Greek amphora is typical of perfume bottles from this period and found throughout the eastern Mediterranean.

This small bronze bottle (top right), inscribed with a dedication by "Amminadab, King of the Ammonites, son of Hissal-el, King of the Ammonites, son Amminadab, King of the Ammonites...for...the vineyards, the gardens, the canals", was found in a Mamluke period earth bank quite close to the surface, suggesting that it may have been admired in private collections for 2000 years.

Bronze bowl (far right) *from Umm Udaina near Amman of a type current in Mesopotamia from the 9th century* BC *onward. An Ammonite inscription just below the lip mentions the former owner, Elshamar. Similar bowls have been excavated from the graveyard at Tell al-Mazar near Deir Alla.*

This incense burner (right) *supported by a caryatid is particular to Jordan. A product of the Syrio-Achaemenid artistic sphere, it has been roughly dated to the 6th century* BC. *The standing female figure with beautifully rendered faces wears the loose garments and jewellery typical of Persian fashions of the day, whilst the stillness of the body and the focus on the head reminds one of earlier Ammonite sculptural traditions.*

taxation was pegged to the gold daric and traffic between the provinces was conducted along royal roads. The Persians also brought with them their state religion, Zoroastrianism, presided over by Ahura Mazda as creator and master of the world. Man, Zoroastrians believed, had the power to decide between good and evil, to choose between truth and untruth. In the end, the world awaited the day of Last Judgement. This new set of moral laws, which subsequently exerted significant influence on all three monotheistic religions, was converted to an idea of political commitment under Darius I (521-486 BC), King of Kings and architect of the vast Persian Empire.

Concurrent with his conquest of Babylonia in 539 BC, Cyrus repatriated the exiled Jews. Jerusalem and its Temple were rebuilt and agricultural communities were re-established. In response, the former kingdoms of Moab and Ammon united one last time, and mounted attacks on Jerusalem to sabotage the resurrections of the city walls. The offensives were led by the Persian-appointed governor Tobias, who had founded a short-lived rogue dynasty based in Rabbath-Ammon. Darius I eventually put an end to the usurper and pledged protection to Jerusalem. Subsequently, a new law was promulgated prohibiting marriage outside of the Jewish tribes. This enmity seems to have been of short duration, however, as there is evidence of substantial Jewish migration into former Ammon in the fourth century BC, and the eventual establishment of the Jewish statelets, Ammonitis and Peraea.

By the beginning of the fifth century BC, the overambitious Persian Empire, which in its prime governed a vast geography comprising most of the eastern Mediterranean from Libya to Lydia, from the Near and Middle East to Northern India and parts of Central Asia, was beginning to fragment. Weakened by uprisings, depleted by continuous confrontations with the Greeks on the one hand and internal intrigues on the other, had left it wide open to the threat brewing in the West. The Macedonian king, Philip II, was planning his own revenge on Persia for its attempts to "enslave" the Hellenistic world. Philip never saw his ambitions fulfilled. In 336 BC, amidst celebrations and flanked by his son and son-in-law, he was assassinated by a disgruntled young Macedonian bodyguard. His son Alexander carried through his father's military ambitions, eventually defeating the Persians in the battle on the Issus River in southeastern Turkey. The year was 333 BC, a date that marks the beginning of the Hellenistic period.

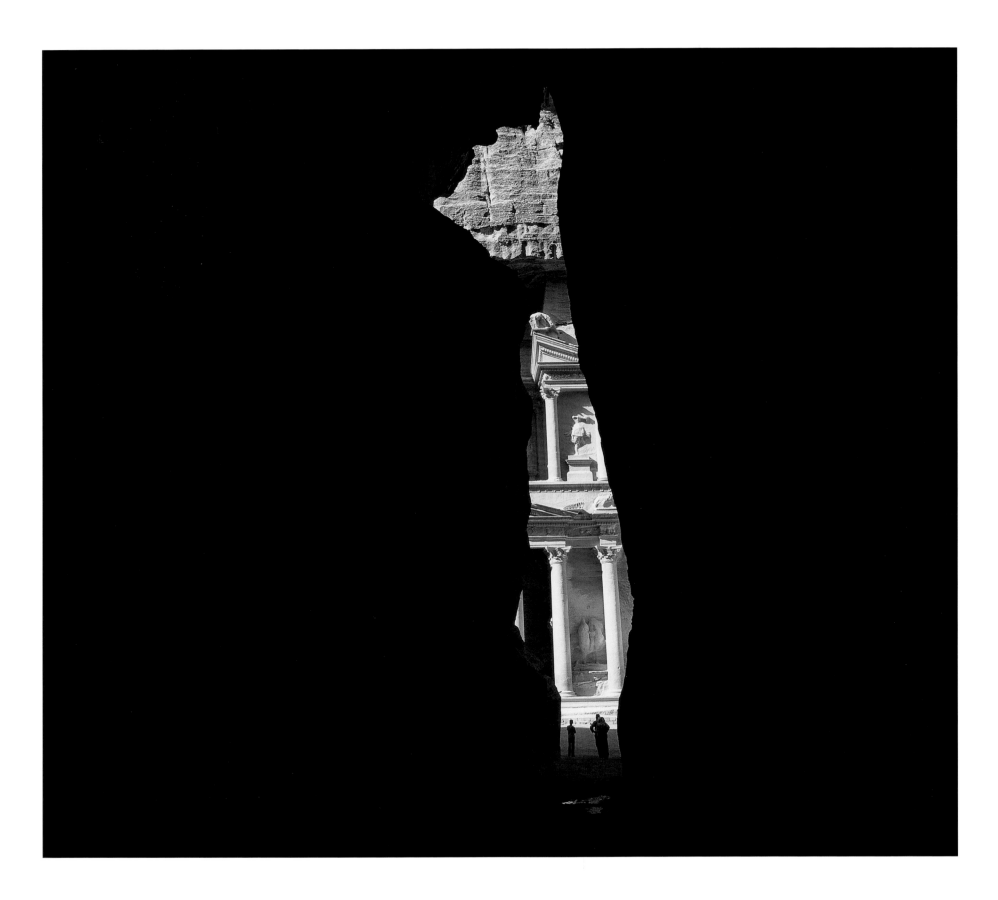

Jordan – A Timeless Land

The Classical Era

In the 13 years between his accession to the Macedonian throne and his untimely death at Babylon in the summer of 323 BC, Alexander the Great had conquered a domain of phenomenal dimensions. Efforts to keep the empire intact, however, soon fell apart. After 40 years of bitter infighting, Alexander's vast dominions were divided into three major kingdoms ruled by Macedonian dynasties headed by his generals: the Ptolemies, with their power base in Egypt; the Seleucids, who assumed supremacy over the vast territories from the Mediterranean to the borders of India; and the Antigonids, who were eventually reduced to the Macedonian heartland and northern Greece. These dynasties, known collectively as the Diadochi, became bitter rivals. From this time of great contest and conflict come the first historical references concerning the founders of Petra, the Nabataeans.

Based on an eyewitness account by the soldier and historian Hieronymus of Cardia, the famous first century BC *Universal History* by Diodorus of Sicily includes a narrative about two armed expeditions by the Antigonids in the years 312-311 BC, against a "certain rock" (Petra/Umm al-Biyara/Sela) and its inhabitants. They were still nomadic, he relates, and skilled in the construction of underground cisterns, permitting quick retreats into the desert with their flocks in times of danger. They were known to trade in aromatics from a wondrous land known to the Greeks as *Arabia Eudaimon*, Arabia the Blessed, and to the Romans as *Arabia Felix* or Happy Arabia. Antigonous' army successfully attacked the "rock" and made off with great booty, but was overtaken by the Nabataeans who massacred all but 50 of the men. In an attempt to persuade the invading Macedonians to leave them in peace, they sent a letter to Antigonous which, significantly, was written in Aramaic, the language of commerce of the day. Over the course of the previous millennium Aramaic, with its 22 consonant-signs, had developed into the Near Eastern *lingua franca*, and had even been utilised by the Persians as the language of commerce and bureaucracy.

In the year of the second attack, Antigonous' son, Demetrios, lost the battle of Gaza against a coalition of Seleucid and Ptolemaic armies. The victors divided their territory between Egypt and India and entered a tug of war over the borderlands on the Mediterranean coast, modern Palestine, Israel and northern Jordan.

Despite the scarcity of historical references during this period, it is almost certain that the Nabataeans benefited from the power vacuum created by those military occupations, enabling the growth of a successful caravan-imperium on the periphery of the hellenised Levant. Half a century after the attacks, the Nabataeans had established commercial centres in the Hauran near the Syrian border, in the Sinai and the Negev, and were controlling the trade into the Hijaz as far as Hegra (Medain Saleh) in Saudi Arabia.

Occasionally they reverted to piracy, and were attacked by Ptolemy II in 278 BC in retaliation for plundering ships bound for Egypt. Two decades later, they are reported to have negotiated commercial sales in the Hauran for a certain Zenon, a Ptolemaic businessman based in Alexandria. Rabel was mentioned as their leader, a name that became synonymous with Nabataean kingship two centuries later.

While the south remained comparatively unaffected by the

The entrance to Petra, the Nabatean rose-red city, is along a narrow gorge or Siq. Visitors are greeted by the imposing facade of the Pharaoh's Treasury, or Khaznat Far'oun.

Lioness relief (left) *and leopard fountain* (right) *still in situ at the Qasr al-Abd. Constructed by Hyrcanus of the influential Tobiad family at the turn of the 3rd to the 2nd BC, the "Fortress of the Servant" epitomises Hellenistic architecture in Jordan*

Macedonian presence, the north was hotly contested by their rivals. Rabbath-Ammon, the once great city of the Ammonites, was in quick succession occupied by Ptolemy I, taken by Seleucus and reconquered by Ptolemy II Philadelphos (285-246 BC), founder of the famous library in Alexandria. Rabbath-Ammon was renamed Philadelphia, "brotherly love", in honour of the Egyptian tradition of sibling marriage. In 198 BC, it was lost once more, this time to the most powerful of all the Seleucid rulers, Antiochus III. Undoubtedly, it owed this attention to its crossroad status. Here, the Mesopotamian and Damascene trade routes met with both the King's Highway and the desert caravan-tracks from the Hijaz, whence commodities were transported across the Jordan River to Jerusalem and Gaza, the great Mediterranean port.

During this period the local dynasty of the Tobiad family which was possibly related to the sixth century BC Persian governor of Ammon (by now well connected in Jerusalem) appears on the scene. Ostensibly serving as administrators under both of the Diadochi kingdoms, they were able to carve out a small sphere of influence against the Seleucids around Philadelphia. Qasr al-Abd, the Palace of the Servant in Wadi Sir some 17 kilometres west of Amman, today stands as the most impressive witness to this period and is a rare example of Hellenistic architecture in Jordan. The massive two-storey palace was once decorated with high reliefs of animals, surmounted by eagles, and surrounded by an artificial lake. Access to the fertile valley was guarded by a military unit housed in an extensive cave complex. Both structures are elaborately described by Josephus in *Jewish Antiquities* VII, along with a short biography of

its owner, Hyrcanus. Apparently, he committed suicide in 175 BC, and the palace was never completely finished.

With the hindsight of the historian, the rivalry between Seleucids and Ptolemies was but a prolongation, under different rulers and with different origins, of ancient antagonisms between the Egyptian, Assyria-Babylonian and Persian empires. In this case, however, while both parties focused on strengthening the trade routes connecting the fledgling Silk Road from China, and the Great Indian Trunk Road with the Iranian Royal Road and the Frankincense Road, both advocated the dissemination of Greek civilisation with interrelated policies. Cities were given the rights of the *polis*, those of free citizens ruled by a Greek upper class and controlled by a council. The strategy throughout the empires was to facilitate assimilation. The population was often augmented by prisoners of war from opposing parts of the empire, creating greater cultural diversity. Mixed marriages were encouraged, and *Koine*, a simplified form of Attic Greek, became the vehicle of government, religion and literature. In Jordan, however, Aramaic remained the primary spoken language, especially in the countryside, long into the Roman era.

The settlements of the fertile north including Pella, Gadara/ Umm Qais and Gerasa/Jarash – the latter was renamed Antioch on the Chrysorhoas by Antiochus IV (175 – 164 BC), a name that never quite caught on – experienced a fate similar to that of Philadelphia/ Amman. Pushed and pulled in the power struggle between the Diadochi it came, along with Palestine, under the hegemony of the Seleucids by the late second century BC. There is little material or

Roughly hewn stepped stone block (left) *with votive niches situated at the far end of the cave complex of Iraq al-Amir, the "Caves of the Prince" which guard the access route to the Qasr al-Abd. Inscriptions link them to the Tobiad family, who kept a military unit there. The historian Josephus allocated significant space to the Hellenistic site in his* Antiquities, *describing the caves in detail* "some for banqueting and others for sleeping and living... and the entrances of the caves, he made narrower so that only one person and not more could enter at one time".

Nabatean votive stele or baitylos (right), *with an inscription reading* "the goddess of Haiyan, son of Nayibat". *Nabatean votive stones of this type, and those of much simpler designs, were influenced by the Arabian religious sphere. Most of them date from the 1st century* BC *and the 1st century* AD.

Naidos! And Greek, Chaire! And you return me the same!"

Gadara faces Lake Tiberias and the Golan Heights and projects like the bow of a great ship over the deep valleys carved out by the Yarmuk and Jordan rivers. A place of natural beauty, it is at once remote from the political centres in the south yet connected to them by its proximity to major roads. After serious disruptions caused by invasions from the Hasmonean ruler Alexander Jannaeus in the early first century BC when most of the intellectual elite went into self-imposed exile, it only regained its reputation as a city of poets and philosophers during the Roman period when it truly flourished.

Even prior to Alexander the Great's triumphal march from Africa to Asia, Greek cultural idioms had been infiltrating the Levantine civilisations, especially to the west of the Jordan River. Local philhellenic movements embraced the new secularism encouraged by the Diadochi, creating in places serious challenges to established orthodoxies. The Old Testament had been translated into Greek by 200 BC, a Jewish community was flourishing in Alexandria and the Samaritans had already separated from Jerusalem in the previous century. Whilst the Ptolemies had consciously pursued a policy of neutrality towards local religious affairs the Seleucids, who had finally wrenched control of Palestine from their rivals in 198 BC, did no such thing. Indeed, they began questioning the Mosaic Laws as the basis for political rule. By the mid-second century, the growing opposition to Hellenism engendered riots against wealthy hellenised Jews. In 169 BC, Antiochus IV marched into Jerusalem, looted the temple, ousted the Zadokian priests and installed the cult of Zeus Olympios/Baal Shamin in their place. The Sabbath was outlawed,

structural evidence from this period apart from the Hyrcanus palace, as many cities settled by the Greeks were extensively re-built and incorporated into the Roman Decapolis federation in the following centuries. A portion of the sanctuary dedicated to Zeus at Jarash is one example; the literary heritage of Gadarene philosophers, poets and witches is another.

Permeated with a sense of relativism that oscillates between the cynical and the Epicurean, between great humour and fine irony, the work of the Gadarene intellectuals during the Hellenistic period mirrors multifarious cultures in an unstable age. Menippus, generally considered the father of philosophical satire, wrote self-mocking, semi-autobiographical dialogues placed in a world which was, in his opinion, quickly disappearing down the River *Styx*. Later, Meleager, a well-known poet-philosopher and contemporary of the famous Gadarene Epicurean Philodemus, summed up the spirit of the day when he wrote: *"If you are Syrian, I say to you Salam! If a Phoenician,*

Along with a large number of piriform cisterns (above), *rock-cut houses and foundations are spread across the plateau of remote Sela rock. First inhabited during the Neolithic period, the natural fortress served as a place for refuge for the Edomites and Nabateans. The Byzantine period saw the construction of a monastery with lofty cells for hermits and holy men. Remnants from the Mamluke period suggest that Sela was occupied until the 14th or 15th centuries.*

(above right) *The largest monumental cuneiform inscription in Jordan can be made out to the left of the staircase. It was probably commissioned by the Babylonian king Nabonidus during his military excursion to Arabia in the 6th century BC.*

the Torah shunned. Heavy resistance from the traditionalists triggered the Maccabean Revolt a year later.

Led by Mattathias of the house of the Hasmoneans, a priest of surprising military talents, the revolution was a success. Under his son, Judas Maccabaeus, it grew into a war of independence of serious proportions, and after the death of Antiochus VII in 129 BC, Seleucid control over Palestine was terminated. Subsequently, Judas' nephew, John Hyrcanus, founded an independent Hasmonean dynasty. In the light of the rapid disintegration of the Seleucid Empire, the later Hasmonean leader Alexander Jannaeus was able to occupy the Hellenistic cities in the north of Jordan from 82 BC onward. Philadelphia/Amman and for a short period the land all the way to the Wadi Hasa, the former border to the Edomite kingdom, also came under Jewish control.

Ironically, because of the unstable political climate, the most important archaeological treasure found in the 20th century was preserved for posterity. In the spring of 1947, Bedouins who had settled near the village of Qumran on the north-western shores of the Dead Sea (officially part of the Hashemite Kingdom from 1950-1967) came upon a cave complex containing a cache of clay receptacles of great antiquity. Some were badly damaged, others filled with complete scrolls in the form of rectangles of kidskin sewn end to end, stored in narrow vessels sealed with bitumen.

Excavations carried out jointly by the French Institute of Biblical and Archaeological Studies and the Jordanian Department of Antiquities between 1949 and 1958, counted 10 complete scrolls, and an additional 50 jars containing more than 600 manuscripts.

Nabatean steps (left) *cut into sheer rock in the Siq al-Barid, a cool narrow gorge near the al-Beidha Neolithic site, and once an active caravanserai on the approach to Petra. The staircase leads to the famous "Painted House", where figures of Pan and Cupid, rendered in a typical eastern Hellenistic style, can still be made out.*

Glass bottle (right) *in the shape of a child's head, a favourite design throughout the eastern Mediterranean during the Roman Era. Double glass bottle* (far right), *probably used for medicinal salves from Abila/Qweilbeh, 4th – 5th century AD.*

Collectively they are known as the Dead Sea Scrolls. Thousands of small pieces were retrieved and transported to Jerusalem where restoration continues to this day.

It was surmised that the manuscripts embodied the intellectual repository of the Essenes, a Jewish sect that grew up in reaction to Judaism tainted by Hellenism, and hidden between the Seleucid persecutions and the final demise of the sect in the early second century AD. They often lived in isolation and hoped to call forth the Messiah by re-establishing the pure heritage of the priesthood, by the practice and interpretation of the Law of Moses and by scrupulous ritual purity. The library comprises documents written in Hebrew, Aramaic and Greek. It includes all the books of the Old Testament, disciplinary and eschatological texts, such as the enigmatic *Conduct of the War Waged by the Sons of Light Against the Sons of Darkness*, as well as reports on the general activities of the sect. Additionally, a number of mysterious copper scrolls in the form of long strips, engraved in the Aramaic "square" script, have come to light. One of these carries a detailed description of 63 separate treasure troves hidden in Palestine weighing a total of 160 tons of gold, silver, ritual implements and other treasures safely concealed from Gentile reach. Some scholars allocate symbolic significance only to the text, whilst others have speculated about the treasure hidden before Antiochus IV sacked the Temple of Jerusalem, an act that led to the expulsion of the Greeks from Palestine.

Trouble had been brewing for some time in the eastern part of the vast Seleucid domain. From the mid-third century BC onward, one of the three Eastern Iranian tribes of the Dahai, the Parni, had been encroaching onto the lucrative trade routes from India and China. They had successfully invaded the Greco-Bactrian kingdoms in what are now Afghanistan and northern Pakistan and rapidly moved west. Far from interrupting the trade, however, they participated vigorously in its expansion. They quickly began to unite Parthia, subsequently founding the Persian Arsacid dynasty (250 BC-224 AD), and within a century were on the way to becoming the most powerful new force in the region. Babylon fell to them in 142 BC and the following year they occupied Seleucia on the Tigris. By 140 BC, the ancient Achaemenid royal title, *Shahanshah*, "King of Kings", had been adopted. A substantial part of the trade route, which was eventually to connect the easternmost termini of the Silk Road with Petra and the Mediterranean, was under their control. Silk was still extremely rare during this time with only small quantities coming across the expanse of the Taklamakan desert and the Karakoram and Hindukush mountain ranges. But there were spices and cottons from India, Scythian gold, carpets and, of course, horses and weapons.

Pressure by the Parthians from the east, by the Armenians in the north and by the Romans who were increasingly demanding their share in the new global trading game, had diminished Alexander the Great's successors' dreams of world domination. With the conquest of Antioch by the Roman general Pompey in 64 BC, the Hellenistic era came to an end. Its legacy, however, was to live on in the cultural, political and social life of the Middle East for centuries to come.

David Roberts, intrepid English explorer and artist, visited Petra in 1839 and recorded in detail every aspect of the rose red city for a captivated audience back home, giving rise to the romanticism that has surrounded Petra ever since.

And he descended through the gorge of ar-Ruba'i which windeth through the mountains to cities amidst most marvellous caves. Those are the houses adorned with columns and gates; the facades are sculpted into the very rock face by carving of chisels, all fretted and friezed into decorative living forms as though they were dwellings for people today. (Excerpt from the Al-Nuwari manuscript nr. 1578, Bibioteque Nationale, Paris, trsl. by Fawzi Zayadine)

By the time this diary entry recounting a visit to Petra by the Mamluke Sultan Baybars on the 28th of May 1276 AD was written, the Nabataean trading empire with its magnificent royal city was all but forgotten. Since its rediscovery by the maverick Swiss explorer Johann Ludwig Burckhardt in 1812, it has commanded the attention of travellers, historians and archaeologists the world over. Although archaeological excavations have been extensive in recent decades, they seem to have barely penetrated the surface of the mysterious site.

Equally nebulous are the origins of the Nabataeans, or *Nabatu*, as they referred to themselves. Over the last century, they have been identified by scholars with the biblical Nebaioth (Genesis 25: 13) and with the Nabaati of the Assyrian chronicles of Assurbanipal (668-631 BC). However, despite superficial linguistic similarities, both theories have since been rejected. Currently, the Nabataeans are thought to have resulted from a schism of the Qedar, a tribal federation mentioned in the Old Testament (Jeremiah 49: 28). In the sixth century BC they are recorded as having aided the Persian King Cambyses in crossing the desert on his way to conquer Egypt, and soon after disappeared from history. It is certain, however, that

following the economic collapse of Edom, nomadic tribes re-settled the region, subsisting on trade and animal husbandry.

Despite the large number of Nabataean inscriptions and graffiti, which have been discovered as far away as southern Italy, Egypt, Arabia, and scattered throughout Jordan, the Negev, Sinai and Syria, an understanding of Nabataean history has come primarily from Greek and Roman sources. Although it is generally accepted that the Arabic script developed from the Nabataean Aramaic, there exist no royal chronicles or administrative records, no private histories or heroic tales. Personal names, blessings, dedications and commemorations scratched into rocks or engraved onto tombs reveal little of the *Saga Nabataea.*

The two most often quoted historians of the time, Diodorus and Strabo, wrote in short succession after one another on either side of the Christian era, at a time when Rome's appetite for exotic luxuries was increasing. Both historians relied on eyewitness accounts. Hieronymus of Cardia's late fourth century BC report paints the picture of a semi-nomadic people skilled in water conservation and involved in the trade of frankincense, myrrh and bitumen – the latter being important to the Egyptian embalming process, and used for caulking ships and boats. Their presence along the Red Sea and in the Hauran was also recorded. Strabo's *Geography* XVI, however, affords a completely different view. Here, a first century BC Petra is depicted as a powerful and cosmopolitan trading centre with many of its monumental building projects under way and ruled over by a king. The narrative relates tales of lavish banquets entertained by singers and of a large number of foreigners in residence. Certainly, by 129 BC, Nabataea had become influential enough to merit a visit by an ambassador from Priene in Asia Minor. Within three centuries the Nabataeans had left their tents and were living in stone houses and finely decorated villas, and had begun creating one of the most enduring architectural testimonies to human ingenuity.

Nabataea had matured in the waning light of Seleucid influence over the region. Around 169 BC, its first king Aretas, is recorded as having granted political exile to the pro-Hellenistic Jewish High Priest Jason (II. Maccabeans 5: 8), a politically motivated act which set the tone for international relations for the next century. It became the Nabataean's militarily most aggressive period in their history.

Successive Nabataean rulers found themselves repeatedly at loggerheads with the Jewish Hasmoneans. In 100 BC Aretas II (ca. 120-96 BC) clashed with Alexander Jannaeus over control of the port of Gaza, while his son Obotas I (96-87 BC) battled against them near

Gadara seven years later. After the death of Antiochus XII, last of the Seleucid rulers on Transjordanian soil, the trade routes to the north were secured. Aretas III (87-62 BC) lost 12 trading centres in former Moab to Alexander Jannaeus, but was able to establish a Nabataean foothold in Damascus at the time. He ruled from Damascus for 13 years, minting coins with the Greek legend "King Aretas Philhellenos", until he was ousted by the Armenian King Tigranes, father in law of the Parthian Shahanshah Mithradates VI, in 72 BC. After the death of Jannaeus, Aretas III attacked Judaea and besieged Jerusalem, but was forced to withdraw by the arrival of the Roman triumvirate Pompey (106-48 BC).

For the northern cities, which had suffered greatly from repeated Jewish invasions, the arrival of the Roman armies must have come as a great relief. Pella had been sacked in 83 BC, ostensibly for refusing to conform to Jewish customs, and a 10-month siege had seriously damaged Gadara. These cities were incorporated into the new Roman Province of Syria, subject to a governor and granted nominal autonomy. Along with Jarash, Philadelphia/Amman, Abila/Quweilbeh, Dion, Damascus and others, they eventually grew into a successful commercial federation known as the *Decapolis*, or 'League of Ten Cities'.

The southern part of Jordan, the Nabataean lands and trading posts did not fare so well at the beginning of Roman rule (64 BC-395 AD). Pompey had pushed them from the periphery of Damascus and had thwarted their siege of Jerusalem. In 62 BC, he commanded his general Aemilious Scaurus to annex Nabataea, and with it the

trade routes to the fabled lands of frankincense and myrrh, *Arabia Felix*. When outright military invasion failed, he besieged Petra, and devastated the outlying agricultural lands. Nabataea paid him off with a tribute of 300 talents of silver, some 6000 kg, and an enormous sum even by today's standards. Eventually they were able to negotiate a degree of autonomy in exchange for tribute payments and, despite loss of territory, expanded their political and commercial influence. Like Nabataea, Judaea also became a client state of Rome.

In 55 BC Crassus, an influential and wealthy member of the First Triumvirate and rival of Pompey and Julius Caesar, proclaimed himself governor of Syria with the ill-disguised ambition to push east. Funded by looting the shrine of the Mother Goddess in Bambice in Northern Syria and the Jerusalem Temple treasure, in the spring of 53 BC he entered northern Mesopotamia at the head of an army of 40,000 men. The campaign proved utterly disastrous for Rome's close-ranked foot soldiers. Confronted by swift Parthian cavalry armed with powerful bows, 20,000 men were massacred at the battle of Carrhae (Haran). Crassus was killed – some say by having molten gold poured down his throat – and 10,000 men were captured and transported east to Merv. To add insult to injury the eagle standards of seven legions were bagged by the "barbarians." Triumphant, the Pathians made Seleucia on the Tigris/Ctesiphon their capital (it was to remain seat of government even under the Persian Sassanids) and crossed the Euphrates into Syria. Their campaign was unsuccessful but came as a warning of things to come for the province.

Remnants of a once luxurious villa incorporating a rare Nabataean bath-complex near the Wadi Rum temple dedicated to the great goddess Allat. Wadi Rum was situated on a major trade route to Southern Arabia, and shows evidence of human activity since the Neolithic Period.

Meanwhile in Rome, Pompey and Caesar had entered into a bitter power struggle, culminating in civil war and defeat for Pompey. He escaped to Alexandria where he was assassinated in 48 BC. Caesar, now absolute master of the Roman world, was hot on his heals. He encircled Alexandria, burnt the Great Library and, beguiled by Cleopatra, made her queen. The Nabataean client-king Malichus I (58-53 BC) sent cavalry to aid Caesar in his Egyptian endeavours, while at the same time secretly supporting the Hasmonean family, and thus the Parthians.

On the 15th of March 44 BC, exactly one month after he was offered (and rejected) the royal diadem by Mark Antony, Julius Caesar was murdered, the result of a plot led by Cassius and Brutus. The conspirators were granted amnesty and, much to the chagrin of Caesar protégé Mark Antony, Cassius proclaimed himself proconsul of Syria, leaving Antipater – Ideomean by birth and father of Herod the Great – in charge of Israel. Cassius began raising funds to fight the new rulers of Rome, the Second Triumvirate, which included Mark Antony and Caesar's grandnephew, Octavian. The job of extorting shekels from the already depleted Jews fell to Antipater, until he was assassinated. A year later (42 BC) Mark Antony and Octavian killed Cassius at the twin battles of Philippi. The empire was subsequently divided between Octavian who received the West, leaving Mark Antony as sole ruler over the eastern provinces. He pronounced Herod and his brother joint Tetrarchs over Israel and parts of Transjordan, and retired to Egypt into the arms of Cleopatra.

Mark Antony had inherited Ceasar's Parthian problem. The problem escalated to a crisis when the Parthian general Pacorus,

aided by a Roman defector, invaded parts of Asia Minor and the Levant. Three centuries after they had been vanquished by Alexander, the Persians once again stood on the shores of the Mediterranean. Jerusalem exploded in civil war, stoked by bitter political intrigues. In fear for their lives, Herod and his family fled from the embattled city in the darkness of night. He sent a messenger to the Nabataean King Malchius at Petra, pleading for asylum and financial support, but was refused. The Parthians had apparently expressly forbidden Nabataean aid to Herod. It was a feeble excuse and one never forgiven. Leaving the women ensconced at his stronghold of Masada, Herod escaped to Egypt, from whence he travelled to Rome. Once there, and contrary to all expectations, the son of an Edomite father and a Nabataean mother was unanimously proclaimed King of the Jews by the Roman Senate.

Within two years of his return to Jerusalem, Herod had eliminated his political rivals and had, predictably, begun to foster his own expansionist ambitions. He marched south to bring Iduemaea back into the fold, and began eyeing Transjordanian real estate. At this same time, Cleopatra in Egypt demanded the lands of the Levant from her lover Mark Antony – and was granted her wish. Cyprus was handed over to her, then the coastal cities and finally the coveted Nabataean copper and bitumen industries.

In the year that he married his beautiful Egyptian queen, Mark Antony gathered an enormous army and marched east into the Caucasus, Armenia and Azerbaijan to confront the Parthians. Not only did he fail to take the ultimate price, the Parthian capital Ctesiphon, but, his supplies lost, his soldiers ill and under attack by

Ad-Deir, "the Monastery", at Petra was probably constructed to commemorate the death of the Nabataean king Obodas I (96-87 BC). He was buried at Obodad (Avdat) in the Negev, and was the first Nabataean king to be deified.

the famed Parthian archers, he was forced to retreat. As his surviving legions recrossed the Euphrates River, the Parthians unstrung their bows, praised the Romans' courage and, waving the captured Roman standards in the air, went home. Humiliated, Mark Antony returned to Egypt to devote himself to Cleopatra and the administration of the Roman East.

Meanwhile, Cleopatra's appetite for land was becoming insatiable. She demanded Jericho, the city of palms and wine and Herod's opulent winter retreat. But Herod was a valuable ally to Antony. To placate her, Antony imposed tax increases on the Nabataeans, to be paid into Cleopatra's coffers. Malichus refused, whereupon Herod was ordered to extract the sum of 200 talents by force. He complied and confronted the Nabataeans at Dion, a Decapolis city on the periphery of the Hauran, and pursued them victoriously – only to be ambushed by a general sent by Cleopatra for that purpose.

Rome had had enough and declared war on Cleopatra, culminating in the battle of Actium and the surrender of 19 of her legions. True to her character, she manipulated Mark Antony into committing suicide, whilst planning to escape via the Red Sea. The Nabataeans, however, thwarted her plans by burning her fleet. Octavian occupied Egypt and seized its enormous treasure with great beneficial effects on the Roman economy. (It is said that the standard interest rate in the empire fell from 12% to 4% as a result of the great booty). Dressed in robes of mourning Cleopatra wrote her last request – to be buried next to Mark Antony – and put an asp to her breast and died.

Octavian set about reconstructing the empire. He enlarged the temple of Apollo at Actium and returned many of the works of art carried off by Cleopatra from cities in the Syrian province. Herod laid his diadem before Octavian's feet, and was duly restored his former holdings won by Cleopatra. Additionally, he acquired Madaba and Machaerus/Mukawir, and built a palace there. He also developed the port at Zara on the eastern shores of the Dead Sea, the baths at Kallirhoë and, much to the dismay of its citizens, was bequeathed the city of Gadara. Some of the Gadarene are said to have committed suicide rather than to be subjected to the tyrant. In the midst of this political chaos, King Malichus I of Nabataea died and was succeeded by Obodas III (30-9 BC).

In 27 BC, command over almost all of Rome's army was placed in Octavian's hands, and soon after he was bestowed the name under which he became known best, Caesar Augustus. Scion of a distinguished banking family, he set about securing the financial well-being of the Roman Empire which now included Egypt, the gateway

to the riches of Africa; and Syria which had become the wealthiest and most important of the imperial provinces. Trade not only flourished again but was increasing to meet the Roman desire for luxuries. The Parthians, however, continued to control access to the Silk Road and the Nabataeans were still the sole middle-men for goods from *Arabia Felix*. Despite the loud voices in Rome calling for reprisals for Crassus' and Mark Antony's humiliations at the hand of the Parthians, Augustus satisfied himself with asserting his authority over Armenia and the Caucasus. Instead, he negotiated peacefully with the Parthian king for the return of the captured legion standards and to fix the border between the two empires on the Euphrates River.

In the south, however, he pursued an altogether more aggressive policy. The most frequented overland route from Arabia now led via the Hijaz to the Nabataean capital of Petra and from there directly to Gaza. Philadelphia/Amman was being sidelined. Augustus had heard about the rock-cut city of *Reqem*, as the Nabataeans called it, from his former tutor the Stoic philosopher Athenodorus, who had at one time resided at Petra. (Strabo based large parts of his Nabataean narrative on Athenodorus.) Now he wanted to eliminate the middle-men and go directly to the source.

The Nabataeans were in a bind. As subjects of a Roman client-state they were obligated to comply with Augustus' orders - tantamount to commercial suicide. However, King Obodas' chancellor Syllaeus, came up with a plan. When the prefect of Egypt arrived at the head of a 10,000-man strong infantry, he offered to guide the expedition. First, he unnecessarily advised the building of a fleet,

The Gadara Decumanus Maximus at sunset. Overlooking Lake Tiberias, the Golan Heights, and situated near the confluence of the Jordan and Yarmuk rivers, Gadara/Umm Qais was an important cultural centre located between major trade routes.

implying that there was no overland route for the first stage of the journey. The Romans complied and, with the addition of 500 men sent by Herod and 1000 Nabataean cameliers, they boarded ship in Aila/Aqaba and headed for the Nabataean port of Leuke Kome. Faulty navigation lost them a number of vessels and troops, and many of the soldiers became ill from water and food supplied by their guides. They were forced to spend the rest of the summer and the following winter in port. In the spring, Syllaeus led the Romans into the desert, far from the trade route with its well-established water cisterns and, avoiding important commercial centres such as Yathrib (Medina). Six months later, after a march that should have taken only two, a bedraggled Roman army arrived at the gates of Marib, capital of the kingdom of Sheba and southern terminus of the Frankincense Road, too exhausted to be able to execute a military manoeuvre. The expedition was deemed a complete disaster. For the time being the Nabataeans were able to keep their monopoly, with Syllaeus as their leading statesman.

Little is known of King Obodas III. Judging by his chancellor's intense involvement in the power-games of the day, however, it seems that he was content to pour wine into golden goblets, while Syllaeus ran the kingdom. In 20 BC, Syllaeus travelled to Jerusalem ostensibly to negotiate a loan from Herod. At a banquet, he caught the eye of Herod's sister, Salome (great-aunt of John the Baptist's nemesis), and returned a few months later to formally ask for her hand in marriage. Herod agreed provided that Syllaeus converted to Judaism, a condition out of the question for the proud Arab. Seething with revenge, he returned to Petra.

Eight years later, while Herod was away on a state visit to Rome, a revolt broke out in his north-eastern province of Trachonitis, the modern Jebel Druze region. When Herod's military dispersed the uprising, Syllaeus granted asylum to 40 of their leaders and provided them with a base to organise raids against Judaea. On his return, the incensed Herod demanded repayment of the loan he had granted years earlier, and the extradition of the brigands. Syllaeus refused and instead went to Rome himself, leaving a votive tablet dedicated to Jupiter Dusares for the safety of his king in the shrine of Apollo at Miletus on the way.

In his absence, Herod destroyed the stronghold of Raepta, the later Ajlun castle north of Jarash, and killed the Nabataean commander Naqib. Informed of the debacle, Syllaeus intrigued heavily at court against Herod. Augustus, who was about to celebrate empirewide peace with the dedication of the *ara pacis augustae* (The Altar of Peace), was furious. In his defence, Herod sent delegations to Rome, when news reached the imperial court that Obodas III had been poisoned and that his nephew Aeneas had taken the crown under the name of Aretas IV (9 BC–40 AD). In the end, Syllaeus was discredited and accused of being instrumental in Obodas' death, the murder of Herod's brother, and even the plot to assassinate Herod. The crafty Nabataean chancellor was arrested and executed.

Under the new king Aretas IV (9 BC–40 AD), Nabataea was to experience its richest and most glorious period. The Khaznat Far'oun, or Pharaoh's Treasury, unrivalled amongst the marvels of Petra and the monument that completely fills ones vision upon emerging from the narrow confines of the *Siq*, was probably

constructed under his reign. As is typical of the eclectic eastern Hellenistic style, it combines architectural elements and iconographic references of various provenances. The Egyptian goddess Isis – star of the sea and patron goddess of travellers, Castor and Pollox, the tutelary divinities of sailors and protectors of hospitality, along with winged victories dominate the theme of the decorations. Viewing the imposing two-storey façade carved into pink-marbled sandstone, the astonished visitor would have been left in no doubt of the wealth and wisdom, perhaps even magnanimity of the ruler. In their many roles, Castor and Pollox were known for secretly testing cities as to the quality of welcome afforded to strangers, but also for accompanying souls on their journey to the underworld. Indeed, the craftsmen of Petra were masters of ambiguity and created many monuments that catered to the polytheistic sensibilities of the time.

The Nabataeans traditionally worshipped deities in aniconic form, represented by steles or roughly hewn rocks called *betyls*. Maximus of Tyre comments as late as the second century AD: "*The Arabs serve I know not whom, but I saw this statue which was a square stone.*" Their principal deity was Dushara, lord of the Shara-mountains to the north of Petra. His consort, Allat, was an ancient Arabian goddess, associated with spring and fertility. She is even mentioned in the Koran (53:19), and together with al-Uzza, the all powerful one, and Manat, the god of destiny, formed a trinity. Writing, so fundamental to Nabataean success, was venerated in the form of Al Kutbay, and Al Qaum, the ancient warrior god who abstained from wine, guarded the caravans. Others, such as Atargatis, the great Syrian sky mother, and Baal-Shamin, originally a Phoenician god, were introduced from the outside and worshipped in high-places, and in the form of *betyls*. All of these deities eventually became affiliated with the major divinities of the Egyptian, Greco-Roman and Syrian religions.

A good example of Nabataean syncretism can be found in the magnificent sculptures from Khirbet Tannur. Located on a mountain top not far beyond the southern escarpment of the Wadi Hasa, the former border between Moab and Edom, Khirbet Tannur served as a sacrificial high-place even before the Nabataeans built a small shrine there in the first century BC. The famous second century white lime-stone temple, however, faces the dark shape of an extinct volcano and overlooks a stretch of the King's Highway. It was dedicated to Atargatis, queen of heaven, and her consort, who has been variously identified with the Greek Zeus, the Egyptian Hadad and the ancient Edomite god Qaws. Although originating in different parts of the world, all three divinities were gods of atmospheric phenomena – of the winds, rain and of thunder, and were always worshipped on mountain tops.

In time we find Allat equated with Athena, sometimes also with Aphrodite, Urania/Venus and al-Uzza with Isis. Dushara takes on aspects of Zeus and Dyonisus, while Al Kutbay is paralleled with Hermes/Mercury, Al Qaum with Aries/Mars, and Manat with Nemesis. Simultaneously, the abstracted, simplistic representations declined (though they were never completely abandoned until far into the Christian era), and gods in human form took their place. Similarly, Assyrian, Greek, Egyptian, even Persian elements were mixed to create a distinctive Nabataean architectural style.

Dhikr et-Tannur, the extinct crater of the volcano facing the Nabataean temple of Khirbet Tannur.

Although their geographical boundaries had been curtailed by Rome, Nabataeans under Aretas IV benefited greatly from Roman hegemony. Not only Petra, but also Hegra, Umm Jimal, Bostra and other trading centres flourished as a result of the great quantities of goods passing through them. Palmyra in Syria began to emerge as a major nexus between Rome and Parthia. Damascus was remodelled and the famous *Via Recta* widened and colonnaded. Previous political disagreements were forgotten, or at least suppressed to the degree that Aretas gave a daughter in marriage to Herod's son Antipas.

In 4 BC, Herod the Great was slowly succumbing to a painful form of arterio-sclerosis, then known as "the king's evil". At about the same time Cyrenius was governor of the Syrian province and called for a census amongst his subjects, prompting Joseph of Nazareth to journey with Mary, to whom he was betrothed, to Bethlehem where she gave birth to Christianity's Messiah. "Wise men from the East", tracking an auspicious comet, found the infant Jesus and bequeathed gifts of gold, frankincense and myrrh on him. (Luke 2: 1; Matthew 2). Shortly after he had ordered the slaughter of the innocent of Bethlehem, Herod died.

His kingdom was divided between his sons Archelaus, who, as main heir and successor to the royal title, received Judaea, Samaria and Iduemaea. He was banished when Pontius Pilate was appointed governor of Judaea (26 TO 36 AD). Herod's second son Philip inherited three of the south-western Syrian counties, whilst the youngest, Herod Antipas, was to rule Galilee and Peraea on the East Bank of the Jordan.

Herod Antipas (4 BC–39 AD) had inherited little of his father's political acumen. Indeed, he is often described as a vain, luxury-loving rogue with a penchant for scandal. Although married to a Nabataean princess, he fell in love and eloped with his brother's wife (granddaughter of Herod the Great) Heroditas. Amongst the Jews, and in the face of ongoing Roman oppression, a number of messianic sects had developed. One such sect, the Essenes (of the Dead Sea Scrolls fame) preached their message of moral decline and impending doom in remote areas. Their most vocal disciple at the time was John the Baptist who had set up a ministry at Beth Avara between the confluence of the Wadi Kharrar and the Jordan River. The unbearable African climate, thick undergrowth and strange wildlife made it a refuge as much as a hermitage. Preaching a return to the rule of law and condemning the Antipas-Heroditas union as sacrilege, John also prophesied the coming of the long awaited saviour – dangerous words in dangerous times. Heroditas was infuriated and arranged the arrest of the preacher. John was brought to Machaerus/Mukawir, the Herodian stronghold and palace overlooking the Dead Sea. The story of Salome's dance, the beheading of the saint and subsequent presentation to Heroditas of his head on a platter, has been famously recounted by Matthew in the New

Testament (14: 2-12). His execution, however, was indicative of a larger movement.

At the same time the newly baptised Jesus of Nazareth began preaching the coming of the kingdom of God and a route to salvation and resurrection on Judgement Day. While his doctrine grew from Jewish religious principles, it added another extremely appealing idea: God had sent his only son in human form to earth. Not much is known about his early life – the last years of his mission are better told by the first four books of the New Testament. However, by the time he had gathered a following of disillusioned Jews around him, Judaea was already on the verge of revolt. Zealots urged non-payment of taxes to the colonisers and advocated the violent over-throw of the regime. A threatened religious orthodoxy tried to hold on to what little power was left to them. The Romans dealt ruthlessly with dissidents, and although he advocated nonviolence and love, Jesus was crucified on charges of blasphemy and sedition during the governorship of Pontius Pilate. Unlike that of any other, however, his crucifixion became integral to the Christian creed, the instrument of his death the very symbol of the faith. His teachings propagated by his earliest disciples, the apostles, quickly gained a popular following, especially amongst the poor and disenfranchised. Persecutions began under the new king of Judaea, Herod Agrippa, and continued during Roman rule. The apostles John and James were beheaded, and Peter, we are told in the New Testament, only escaped by divine intervention. Christians, unless they recanted, were punished by law and regularly subjected to slave labour. Many died in mines such as Wadi Feinan, south east of the Dead Sea.

Third century AD olive press (left) *located near the South Gate at Jarash, the ancient Gerasa. Olive cultivation in Jordan dates back to the late Neolithic period, providing produce both for local consumption and for export.*

Hadrian's Gate (right) *was built to commemorate the Roman emperor's visit to Jarash in 129-30 AD, when he wintered in the city. Known as the 'travelling emperor', Hadrian was particularly fond of Rome's eastern provinces and undertook extensive journeys to supervise their administration. His reconstruction of Jerusalem as the colony of Aelia Capitolina led to the famous Bar Kochba revolt, culminating in the banning of Jews from Jerusalem in 133 AD.*

The days of the Herods were numbered, as were those of the Nabataeans. In 37 AD, Aretas IV destroyed Herod Antipas' army purportedly to avenge his daughter's honour. Soon after, Aretas died and was succeeded by Malchius II (40-70 AD). Not much is known of him other than his contributions of arms and troops to quell the first Jewish uprising in Jerusalem, a bloody war that raged for three years in reaction to Nero's insistence on the cult of the Emperor and the building of an imperial shrine. Jerusalem was destroyed in 70 AD, a year which also coincides with Malchius' death. Machaerus fell the next year, and the rebels ensconced in the hill-top fortress of Masada, just a quarter of a mile west of the Dead Sea, held out for another two years. *Iduea capta*, read the legend on the newly minted Roman coins, commemorating the defeat. A number of Christians fleeing from the embattled province found refuge in Pella, which became home to the first Christian communities in present-day Jordan.

Meanwhile, the demand for aromatics produced in Arabia and shipped through Transjordan had never been higher. The emperor Nero was said to have burnt an entire year's harvest of frankincense at the funeral of his wife. Control of the trade routes to the south had become inevitable. Rome had never forgotten its humiliation by Syllaeus, and had been slowly usurping the Nabataean trade monopoly by building up its own merchant navy in the Red Sea. Additionally, incursions by nomadic Bedouins into the Sinai and the Negev were weakening the southern districts. The last of the Nabataean kings, Rabel II, moved his capital to Bostra, where he was able to sustain Nabataean wealth, building the renowned Nabataean

Gate to commemorate his reign. In 106 his trading empire was annexed by Rome's new governor to Syria, Cornelius Palma (in exchange for Roman citizenship, it has been suggested) and incorporated into Rome's newly established Province of Arabia. Coins were minted with the legend *Arabia adquista* not *capta*, specifying an acquired not captured Arabia. The Roman Empire, with Trajan (98-117) on the throne had reached its absolute zenith of power.

The new Arabian province encompassed former Nabataea and the Jordanian Decapolis cities in the north. Bostra received the title *Nova Traiana*, and Petra was granted the status of *metropolis*. In 111-114, the King's Highway was renovated and extended by the governor Claudius Severus and under it's new name *Via Nova Traiana*, connected Aila/Aqaba on the Red Sea with Bostra, just 27 kilometres north of the modern border between the Hashemite Kingdom and Syria. It formed the backbone of Roman Jordan. Garrisons, forts and

*Head of Zeus-Serapis from Gadara/
Umm Qais, second half of the
2nd century AD.*

Charax into a client state. There, the master of the *orbis Romanus*, stood on the shores of the Persian Gulf and gave homage to Alexander, while dreaming of India. In the year of his death 117 AD, the unified Roman Empire extended from the British Isles to Morocco, from eastern Armenia to Egypt, encompassing the entire Mediterranean and its hinterlands. Its *limes* fortified the perimeters of the Sahara and the Arabian deserts, and Roman merchant ships sailed the seas of the known world.

Jordan's role had been, as so often in history, reduced to that of a buffer against incursions from the desert and a nexus to facilitate trade (and military mobility), its fortunes linked to that of the leading superpower. The north provided agricultural products, primarily wheat but also olives, oil and wine, feeding the Roman troops dispersed throughout the East, whilst the southern copper and bitumen industries still contributed substantially to the national economy. For the average citizen, life did not appear to change significantly. A collection of manuscripts deposited in a cave at around the time of the Bar Kohkba revolt, affords rare insight into the life of a Jewish woman named Babatha who resided south of the Dead Sea. The documents range over several decades and represent court records concerning property, guardianships, gifts, marriages and the like, litigated at Petra and Rabbath-Moab/Rabba. Both Greek and Nabataean-Aramaic is used, and at some point oaths sworn to the king are replaced by those sworn to the emperor. The names and details appearing in the documents, however, testify to a multiethnic community living at close quarters with one another and subject to the same laws.

watchtowers, spaced at a distance of 20 kilometres from each other, protected commerce and agricultural lands attached to market towns. More importantly, it facilitated the speedy movement of troops. Nabataean cameliers and horsemen were integrated into the imperial army, and were used to strengthen the frontiers to the east, where the *Limes Arabicus* was to secure the province.

Trajan had finally subdued and assimilated the kinglets and client states around the empire, when trouble was once more brewing in the Parthian domain. This time, the Roman emperor did not resort to negotiation. Fresh from his triumph in Dacia, he moved east, took the Parthian client state of Adiabene and renamed it the Province of Assyria. With boats that had been dragged across the desert in a phenomenal feat, he descended the Tigris, besieged Ctesiphon and carried off the Shahanshah's daughter and the famous golden throne of the Parthians. Trajan then pushed downstream, turning Mesene with its important trading centre of Spasimu

The inner sanctuary of the temple of Artemis, patron goddess of Jarash. Virgin goddess of the moon and the hunt, she was also the protector of women in labour, of small children and wild animals. Devotees would approach this splendid temple by a monumental stairway of seven times seven steps, offering gifts and prayers at a larger altar near the sanctuary. A second altar was reserved for a select few, while only priests were allowed to enter the inner sanctum.

After Trajan's death his nephew and adopted son Hadrian (117-38) ascended the imperial throne. Essentially peaceful, he returned the princess and the golden throne to the Parthians and personally set about simplifying the administration of the empire, undertaking long and arduous journeys across his realm. He clarified the legal system, instituted city constitutions throughout the East and fostered urbanisation by presenting civic structures to communities, thus invigorating local economies as well as reinforcing loyalty to the empire. On the site of the demolished Jerusalem he founded a new city, Aelia Capitolina, and began constructing a temple dedicated to Jupiter where the former Jewish Temple once stood.

Led by Simeon bar Kosiba, hailed as the Messiah and referred to as Bar Kochba (Son of a Star), the Jews united in revolt one last time. The rebellion began in 132, ousting the Roman Xth Legion, leaving Bar Kochba to establish a provisional government. Confident of his victory, he began minting coins with the legend "Year One of the Redemption of Israel" and set up an altar on the Temple site. Hadrian's general Sextus Julius Severus, who had distinguished himself in Britain, was chosen to solve the problem. He did so ruthlessly. By 135 AD Jewish Jerusalem was no more. Aelia Capitolina was repopulated with non-Jewish citizens, and Jews were allowed to visit the city only once a year to mourn at the Wailing Wall. With the renaming of Judaea as *Syria Palestinae*, a Diaspora began for the Jews that was to last for almost two millennia. As had been the case during previous pogroms, Jordan provided refuge to Jewish communities in exile.

Under the mantle of the *Pax Romana* Pella, Gadara, Philadelphia/Amman and many other cities and towns throughout Jordan flourished. Gerasa/Jarash became one of the wealthiest provincial cities of the empire. An ambitious building program, which had commenced under Trajan, was continued vigorously by Hadrian and his immediate successors, heralding a Golden Age for Rome's Arabian province that was to last until the beginning of the third century.

In commemoration of Hadrian's visit to Jarash in 129-30 (during the same visit Petra received the title of *Hadriana Petra Metropolis*) a great triumphal arch was erected half a kilometre to the south of the city, indicating plans for further extensions of the expansive site. The city was completely redesigned around 150, motivated by the construction of a temple dedicated to Artemis, the patron goddess of Jarash. Considered the most beautiful architectural structure amongst the opulent public buildings at Jarash, the sanctuary was approached by a sacred way from the east, a triple arched entrance and a monumental stairway of seven times seven steps. Offerings were made to the daughter of Zeus and twin sister of Apollo on a series of altars – while the holy of holies was accessible only to her priests. Under the governorship of Geminius Macianus (162-66) Philadelphia/Amman received its magnificent Temple of Hercules and a few years later the largest theatre in Jordan, just below Amman's citadel hill, was completed. Renowned for its excellent acoustics, the theatre could accommodate 6000 spectators and is still in use today. Similarly, most of the standing structures at Gadara hail from this period, and once again poetry, learning and philosophy

This delightful bronze lamp (far left) *in the form of a duck was found at Karak, and is representative of a type enjoyed in the late Roman period. Note the heads and arms of two children peeking through the feathers on the side of the neck. Animal representations* (left) *continued as part of the artistic vocabulary far into the Islamic period and were often expertly executed. This detail from a river scene is part of an intricate mosaic floor in the church of SS. Lot and Procopius at Khirbet al-Mukhayyat, and has been dated to the 6th century* AD.

flourished and excelled in the city above Lake Tiberias.

Roman control of the Red Sea and its expansion into the Indian Ocean trade, which had increased dramatically with the discovery of the monsoon winds, was taking its toll on the overland routes. Additionally, much of the Middle Eastern trade was being redistributed via Palmyra, the trading oasis in eastern Syria, rather then by the way of Petra. Economic recession throughout the Arabian Peninsula caused renewed waves of migration towards Transjordan, while the disintegrating Parthian Empire gathered its strength to challenge Rome once more. In reaction, the Western Legions were sent to Syria and defensive systems along the desert periphery were strengthened; the Azraq oasis, terminus for traffic arriving up the Wadi Sirhan, was fortified.

Rome never lost its desire for controlling the trade routes approaching the riches of the East. Emperor Lucius Verus (130-169) once again invaded the buffer state of Armenia, turned west and took Seleucia. Attack followed counterattack, until in 199 Septimus Severus, emperor of Rome from 193-21, was able to lay his hands on the ultimate price: the Parthian seat of power, Ctesiphon.

Severus, a native of Africa and distinguished soldier had married one of the great women of the East, Julia Domna, the 17-year-old daughter of the High Priest of the Sun at Emesa in 187. (Her sister Julia Maesa and niece Julia Mamaea both gave birth to future emperors). Six years later, Severus was declared ruler of the Roman Empire, thus famously fulfilling a prophecy foretelling that Julia would wed a king.

The royal couple embodied a new type of eastern Roman aris-tocracy. Neither of them had been born in Europe, indeed Julia felt passionately Syrian. Both were highly educated and Julia held a literary salon that saw some of the most famous names of the age. Aelian and the Emperor-to-be Gordian, Philostratus, Serenus and the physician-philosopher Galen, all argued, sang and thought for the pleasure of the beautiful empress. Together, the couple dominated the Roman world culturally as much as militarily for 18 years and had two sons. Caracalla, the first born, murdered his brother a year after their father's demise in York in 211. Severus' dying words famously instructed his sons to *"enrich the soldiers and despise the rest of the world"*. With Julia as co-regent, Caracalla continued to rule until 217 and endeavoured to occupy Mesopotamia, Arbela and part of Medea. He was finally defeated by the Parthians at the battle of Nisibis, shortly after which he was assassinated. Julia died the same year and was later deified.

The Roman Empire was beginning to deteriorate, while in many eastern courts the adoption of "oriental" habits, clothing and etiquette was preparing the way for a Byzantine *modus vivendi*.

In the East a new power was on the rise, threatening the Roman defences with renewed vigour. For some time the people of the southern Iranian province of Pars, had been trying to overthrow Parthian domination. Uniting under Ardashir I (224-240), the Sassanids (224-651) set about reviving ancient Iranian ideologies and the dream of its long lost Persian Empire. Petty kingdoms and principalities were centralised around the "King of Kings" who ruled over a society rigidly divided into four classes: priests, warriors, secretaries and commoners. Zoroastrianism was adopted as the state

Late Roman glass objects from graves in Majayy, a small village east of Karak.

religion, with the priesthood exerting enormous political power.

Both Roman emperors Gordian III and Philip the Arab fought against the new Persian Dynasty. Nonetheless, in 256, the Sassanids captured Dura Europos, the wealthy trading oases west of the Euphrates and nexus for goods shipped to Palmyra and Damascus. In 260 Shapur I (240-272) contrived – some say by treachery, others say by battle – to capture the Roman Emperor Valerian, a feat that has been famously chiselled into Persian history on the rockface at Naqsh-e Rostam. Valerian died in captivity while Shapur blazed into Syria and Cappadocia, leaving behind a trail of destruction. On his return to Ctesiphon he was attacked by the client-king of Palmyra, Odaenathus

Palmyra traditionally facilitated trade between Dura Europos and Damascus, and on the whole favoured commerce over military entanglement. Nonetheless, Palmyra possessed a crack regiment of archers By successfully pursuing Shapur, Odaenathus rose to be the leading military figure in the East. On his assassination in 267, his wife Zenobia (Bat Zabbai) took the throne and separated Palmyra from Rome. Zenobia displayed political ambitions not seen since Cleopatra and set about absorbing the Roman East. For a short time she incorporated the Province of Arabia (Jordan) and drove her troops all the way to Egypt. With some difficulty, the Emperor Aurelian was able to force her back to Palmyra, where he found desert tribes attacking from behind in aid of the Arabian warrior-queen. Eventually, she was captured and granted amnesty. It is said that she married a Roman governor and retired to a villa near Tivoli. Significantly, the appearance of a small number of Arab states on the periphery between Sassanid Persia and Eastern Rome date from this time.

The fall of Palmyra left a power vacuum that was immediately filled by the South Arabian overland route. Caravans loaded with frankincense and myrrh, China silk and India spices, once more flowed through Aila/Aqaba, the Kings Highway and the Wadi Sirhan. Measures to protect the diverted traffic were needed. Subsequently, Lejjun, the Roman fortress of the *Legio IV Martia*, between Qatrana and Karak was constructed by Diocletian (284-305), who also extended the road system between Azraq and Damascus – the *Strata Diocletiana*.

Diocletian was vehemently anti-Christian (the famous story of the "Cave of the Seven Sleepers" (HK Sura 18), at a site near Amman, is placed in this period) considering Christianity a threat to the very existence of the Roman Empire. His persecutions created some of the first Jordanian martyrs of the church, and one can assume that his reorganisation of the province was motivated by an attempt to counter internal unrest. Petra and the land all the way to the Wadi Hasa, as well as the Negev and part of Sinai were incorporated into the province *Palestinae*, while the northern part of the Province of Arabia retained its old name. Ammianus Marcellinus, the last of the great Roman historians, describes a fourth century Jordan, where wild tribal men in colourful clothing on fast horses and slim camels roamed the desert periphery, while its *"great cities, Bostra, Gerasa and Philadelphia,* (were) *strongly defended by mighty walls."*

Despite severe persecution under Diocletian's rule, Christian converts were multiplying throughout Jordan using secret symbols,

Central octagonal hall of the Byzantine church complex at Gadara with floor tiles echoing the architectural plan.

such as fish crafted from glass or clay, to identify each other (the Greek **ICHTHUS** "fish" is an acrostic *for Iesous Christos Theou Uiou Soter*). At the same time, Roman religious cults became progressively orientalised. Mithra, Isis, or the all-encompassing Sun, had been slowly replacing the old gods, thus providing a transition to the new faith centred on the "Anointed One". Christianity had first spread by way of the Jewish Diaspora and by trade, as well as through the military stationed in the east. By the end of the second century, the writings of the Apostolic fathers had become standardised to form the basis of a new monotheistic religion with a hierarchical church structure.

Diocletian's death spawned two decades of civil war between the newly created eastern and western administrations, which only came to an end when Flavius Valerius Constantinus, known in history as Constantine the Great (274-337) was declared sole emperor. On the 11th of May 330, holding a sceptre in one hand and an orb with a fragment of the "True Cross" (miraculously retrieved from Jerusalem by his mother Helena three years earlier) in the other, Constantine formally dedicated the city of New Rome to the Holy Virgin. Under Theodosious (379-395) Christianity was adopted as the state religion, and the Roman Empire was officially divided into its western and eastern parts, with Rome remaining the capital of the west and Constantinople the New Rome of the east. A "friendship accord" with the Sassanid Shahanshah Shapur III (383-388) inaugurated a period of uneasy peace between the two archrivals, and incidentally brought some relief to the persecuted Christian communities in Iran. In 476 Rome fell to the Ostrogoths, leaving a

Newly excavated octagonal sanctuary at Gadara, possibly a Roman period mystery temple.

thriving Greco-Roman Byzantine Empire as the sole inheritors of classical civilisation.

For Jordan the Byzantine era (395-636) was one of great prosperity. Never before, and not again till the latter part of the 20th century, was the country so densely settled. Fortified villages near military installations in the east and along the caravan routes protected inter-regional and international trade, while agriculture was expanded in the north. Field terracing, innovative irrigation systems, as well as planned reforestation are still visible on the western slopes of the Jordanian highlands, with the plains around Madaba and Hesbon also intensely cultivated. The construction of Christian churches was encouraged and supported by the state, and a large number of former pagan temples were renovated and reconsecrated. Monasteries were built on holy sites such as Jabal Haroun, Mt. Nebo, on Mar Elias, in isolated hermitages such as the Sanctuary of Lot, and throughout the Jordan valley, catering to local converts as well as to an increasing flow of foreign pilgrims.

True to Diocletian's predictions, the church replaced all classical institutions. A number of towns and cities throughout Jordan became bishoprics, answering to Constantinople. By the fifth century, the Byzantine Empire was divided into seven administrative regions with Jordan belonging to the wealthy Diocese *Oriens*, which reached from former Nabataea to northern Syria and included the Levant littoral and Cyprus. No less than 15 Byzantine churches have been excavated at Madaba thus far, each one decorated with intricately laid mosaics. Wadi Feinan, the Roman and Byzantine Phaino,

became a bishropic and saw an increase in copper production and the expansion of the Roman settlement there. Umm Jimal built numerous churches and a cathedral on a similar pattern repeated throughout Jordan.

In Petra, where Diocletian's persecution had been severe, Christianity only slowly regained a foothold, inciting the famous church historian and Constantine biographer Eusebius (260-340) to complain about pagan cults there. In the mid-fifth century, Petra came under the jurisdiction of the Patriarch of Jerusalem, and was elevated in status to one of the three metropolitan bishoprics in *Palestinae*. Apparently, it now served as a place of banishment for church apostates, the most famous of whom was the former Nestorian patriarch of Antioch. Nonetheless, a church with some of the most impressive mosaics in Jordan has been excavated there, along with papyri scrolls recording the economic and social life of the community from 528-582. The 84 mosaic medallions frame animal and human representations, personifications of the four seasons, wisdom, earth and the oceans. Together with the destroyed wall mosaics, which would have illustrated religious scenes and the heavens, they are a rare example of man's attempt to illustrate all God's domain. By now Petra had become a place of exile, not yet abandoned, but a mere shadow of its former glorious past.

Change in funeral customs from cremation to inhumation had decreased the demand for frankincense throughout the New Rome, precipitating further economic decline in the fragrance producing areas of Southern Arabia. This in turn fuelled the already creeping recession throughout the Arabian Peninsula and caused new waves

(527-65) in 529, and in a client-relationship of the type previously held by the Nabataeans, the Ghassanids patrolled the desert periphery. The frontier tribes of the Christianised Arab Lakhmids entered into a similar association with the Sassanids.

Despite repeated negotiations and ceasefire agreements, the Byzantine and Sassanid empires continued to exhaust each other with skirmishes or outright battles. Justinian and Khosro I (531-579), both hailed as great rulers in their own time, negotiated "eternal peace" in 532. It only lasted a few years, when in 540 Khosro used the pretext of a quarrel between Ghassanids and Lakhmids to besiege the great city of Antioch.

Two years later the first great pandemic plague arrested all activities, military and commercial alike. Carried along trade routes by ship and by land, the plague rampaged from Egypt into Africa, from the Byzantine Empire into Europe, the Middle East and into Asia, killing an estimated quarter up to a third of the population. Justinian himself was stricken, leaving the administration of his shaky empire in the hands of his wife Theodora. He survived and once more negotiated with the Sassanids. Peace was agreed again in 561, laying down terms for freedom of trade and religion between the two opposing empires. It lasted for four decades, and inaugurated a period of growth and prosperity for Jordan.

In 602, the Sassanids launched a major offensive against Byzantium. Eight years later the young Heraclius and his African forces were welcomed by the imperilled city of Constantinople. His reign (610-641) was to be marked by pivotal changes in the political landscape of the Middle East.

of economic migrants to penetrate the peripheral areas between the "desert and the sown". Subsequently, many of these migrant-communities adopted the new faith and were absorbed by the Diocese. One such confederation of tribes, the Ghassanids from Yemen, eventually were able to expand their power base from Syria into parts of Jordan. Its king was formally recognised by the Byzantine Emperor Justinian

Byzantine ruins at Umm Jimal (left), *a black basalt city near the Syrian border. It was first settled as a Nabatean staging post en route to Bostra, and was linked to the* Via Nova Traiana *during the Roman and Byzantine periods, when it truly flourished. Most of the remains are from the 5th and 6th centuries, when numerous churches were built. It continued as an important trading city into the Islamic period, but was destroyed by earthquakes in the 8th century. (CP)*

Sixth century mosaic medallion (right) *from the Apostle's Church, Madaba, depicting a personification of the sea. The inscriptions dedicates this masterpiece to Anastasius, Thomas and Theodora, and identifies the artist as one Salaman. (DoA)*

In the very year of Heraclius' accession to the throne of the Eastern Roman Empire, Mohammed, a merchant from the tribe of the Quarysh, began preaching messages related to him by the angel of God in the south-west Arabian oasis of Mecca. His teachings of the one God and His Judgement Day, of reward and punishment in heaven and hell, lent on the pervading Jewish and Christian religious traditions of the time, and resonated deeply with the traders and pastoralists of the desert. Not all of the Quarysh, who adhered to beliefs similar to that of the Nabataeans, however, received his message with a kind ear.

By 613, the Persians had reached Damascus again. Then, one by one, the great cities fell to their armies. Antioch, Aleppo, Jarash and the fertile north of Jordan were sacked. By 614, the Persians had extended their influence to the southern part of the empire and laid siege to Jerusalem. The Church of the Holy Sepulchre was burnt and the True Cross was seized together with other relics of the Passion of Christ, and carried off to Ctesiphon. Within two years they were back in Egypt. Transjordan, already decimated by plague and war, declined during the 15 years of Persian rule. Finally, on Easter Monday 622, Heraclius began a counteroffensive and in a six year campaign succeeded in driving the Sassanids from Byzantine territory.

The Prophet Mohammed and his first followers meanwhile had moved from Mecca to Yathrib (Medina – The City) in the same year. This event is known in Islam as the *Hijra*, and later designated the beginning of the Muslim era, with a calendar distinct from the Christian measure of years. In Medina Mohammed established an *umma*, a community of followers, and engaged in armed struggle with the Quarysh, ostensibly for religious reasons but possibly over control of the trade routes. He began forging political alliances with Arab tribes on the periphery of the desert, including those settled in the border areas of Transjordan.

In September of 628, Heraclius returned victoriously from battle against the Sassanids, carrying the True Cross before him, with the first elephants ever seen in Constantinople in his wake. The following spring, accompanied by his wife, niece and eldest son, he journeyed to Jerusalem, personally carrying the True Cross along the Via Dolorosa to the restored Church of the Holy Sepulchre. Unaware of his impending doom, he returned to the eastern provinces to reorganise the administration and to address some of the doctrinal problems threatening to divide the Christian church.

In his absence, the Arab tribes of the Jordanian desert areas, now allied to Mohammed, attacked Mu'ta near Karak, a Byzantine garrison which had been established to keep check on tribal migrations. They were repelled. A second attack, this time with reinforcements from Medina was also resisted by the garrison, claiming its first Muslim martyrs. Jafar Abu Taleb, Zaid ibn Haritha and Abdullah ibn Ruaha all lay buried at Mazar south of Karak. According to history, the Prophet was planning a third, large-scale military expedition on his death. Before he died, he sent a series of letters to neighbouring heads of state, inviting them and their subjects to submit to the one true faith of Islam.

Jordan – A Timeless Land

The Early Islamic Era

The Prophet Mohammed died of fever on the 8th of June 632, leaving no clear instructions for his succession. A consensus amongst the inner circle of early followers passed the leadership of the *umma* to his most trusted lieutenant and father-in-law, Abu Bakr, who assumed the title of Caliph (successor/deputy). He did so over another contender, Ali, the Prophet's beloved cousin and husband of his daughter Fatima.

Persia and Byzantium were fatigued and locked in a political stalemate, a state of affairs ultimately of benefit to the newly resurgent Arabs. India and China trade was once again conducted along the desert transit routes and the Red Sea, infusing the impoverished lands of former *Arabia Felix* with revenue. Moreover, for the first time in its history, the diverse tribes of the Arabian Peninsula had united under one leadership and one religion, propagated by one book: Mohammed, Islam and the Holy Koran.

The rapidity of the Muslim advance – and its longevity – was unprecedented in world history. In 633, a virtually unknown people erupted from the desert. A year later, and it seems, with little resistance from the local population, they had taken the Transjordanian highlands. Abu Bakr died in 634 and Omar assumed the leadership as the second Caliph. During his 10 year rule, Islam's first great victories were won.

Under the military command of Khalid ibn al-Walid, the Muslim armies captured Amman and Damascus and laid siege to Jerusalem. Although Heraclius contrived to organise a counterattack and drove Walid back to the Yarmuk River, the present northern border of the Hashemite Kingdom, final victory eluded him. On the 20th of August 636, a violent storm blew in from the south and Walid charged into battle. Blinded by desert winds laced with sand, the Byzantine troops were massacred. A defeated Heraclius was smuggled into Jerusalem where he removed the True Cross and returned with it to Constantinople, while the remainder of the Byzantine army was forced to retreat to Anatolia. Five years later, Heraclius died a broken man. Omar returned to Damascus and installed a governor from the Meccan Umayyad family. Jerusalem capitulated to Muslim armies in February 638, its Christian population watching in silence as Caliph Omar rode into their Holy City on a snow-white camel.

By now Jordan, Palestine and all of Syria were under Arab jurisdiction. Soon Egypt and Armenia would follow, then the Empire of Sassanid Persia, Afghanistan and most of the Punjab. By the time Othman, the third caliph and a member of the powerful Umayyad family, assumed leadership of the *umma* in 644, Muslim armies had gained control over the trade routes from the Sahara to northern India.

During the rule of the first three caliphs (also known as the orthodox caliphs), the capital of the new Islamic empire was maintained at Medina. This changed with the investiture of the Prophet's cousin Ali as fourth caliph in 656, who moved his government to Kufa, in what is now Iraq. Ali's accession, however, was disputed by a number of dissentient groups, but above all by the governor of Syria, Muawiya of the Umayyad family. Factions formed on both sides around the two men and civil war threatened to dissolve the new empire in its infancy.

Just off the King's Highway rises Shobak Crusader Castle, the former Mons Realis (Montreal).

The conflict was put to arbitration in Urdruh, a former Roman military castle on the *limes* between the desert oasis of Ma'an and the Kings Highway north of Shobak, but the issue was left unresolved. When Ali was assassinated by a disgruntled former follower and member of a radical religious sect, Muawiya assumed the caliphate and moved the centre for religious and political authority to Damascus. Consequently, Ali's eldest son formed a short-lived rival caliphate in presnt-day Iraq, but was persuaded by majority consensus to abdicate. This is generally considered the impetus for the political schism between Sunni, those who accept the legitimacy of the first three caliphs, and the Shia, who recognise Ali as the rightful successor to Mohammed.

After Muawiya's death in 680, a second civil war, incited by Ali's second son Hussein, shook the young empire. His defeat at Karbala in Iraq provided the Shiites with their greatest martyr and shrine. Along with the holy cities of Najaf (the site of Ali's tomb), Samarra and Kazimayn near Baghdad, it grew into a thriving centre of Shia learning, attracting students from throughout the Muslim world.

Today, most Jordanian Muslims base their *sunna*, path or practice, on the orthodoxy of the "Six Books" of traditions. Shiites, or the Party (*Shi'atu*, later simply Shia) of Ali, account for only a small minority. Both draw their belief and religious practice from the same koranic source. All Muslims must adhere to the "Five Pillars" of Islam: profession of faith, ritual prayer, payment of alms, fasting during the month of Ramadan and pilgrimage (*Hajj*) to Mecca. Shiites, however, invest more power in the Imams, their spiritual leaders. (An example of a majority Shia country today is Iran). Most Jordanian Shiites are known as 'Twelver Shiites', recognising a succession of 12 Imams from Ali, and believing that the last, or "hidden" Imam who disappeared in 878 will reappear on Judgement Day as the *Mahdi*, the rightly guided one who will rule the earth by divine will.

In the Umayyad Period (661-750) Jordan benefited greatly from its geographical position between Damascus, the political centre and Mecca, the spiritual heart of the new caliphate. During the Arab conquest, maritime trade in the Mediterranean and the Red Sea had come more or less to a stand still and the overland routes were revived. Its proximity to *al-Quds*/Jerusalem, as well as being traversed by the *Darb al-Hajj*, the pilgrimage route to Mecca, provided additional revenue.

Byzantine administrative structures were only slowly displaced by Arabic ones, and Greek, the language of bureaucracy, was phased out over several generations. The land was divided between two of the five Syrian *ajnad*, or administrative regions: to the north-west lay the Jund of Damascus, while the Jund of Jordan extended from Amman to Aqaba. In the late ninth century, the latter was incorporated into the Jund of Palestine, with the town of Ramla as its administrative centre.

Late Byzantine-early Islamic period bronze and iron brazier found in a cache of artefacts on the western periphery of Mafraq. Displaying Greco-Roman as well as Iranian stylistic elements, this beautiful object exemplifies the eclectic tastes of the time.

The Islamic Empire continued to expand. By 711, it had occupied the entire North African coast and was moving inland to control the lucrative trans-Saharan trade, while threatening the African Sahel kingdoms. With the support of African Berber tribes, the Arabs invaded Spain and by 732 had crossed the Pyrénées and were heading north towards the banks of the Loire, ready to take the European heartland.

On the whole, the Umayyads pursued a policy of integration, granting religious freedom to Christian and Jewish communities, who shared in the new economic prosperity. Taxation proved mightier than the sword and membership of the new faith grew accordingly. A prohibition on translating the Holy Koran facilitated the spread of the Arabic language throughout the new Islamic world, providing a new *lingua franca* for trade from Spain to Central Asia, from Africa to Malaysia. Nonetheless, it appears that the Christian population in Jordan was not significantly reduced until, or shortly before, the Crusades (1097-1291). Indeed, semi-autonomies were granted under *archons* who maintained relations with the church in Constantinople, and Christian religious structures continued to be built and magnificently embellished. Irrigation was controlled and sustained by the new state and special attention was given to the development of agriculture, while wine production flourished.

Rather than rejecting the cultural legacies of the countries which they occupied, the Umayyads adapted through cultural synthesis and thus created some of the most enduring legacies to Islamic art and architecture. The Damascus Mosque, the Dome of the Rock on Jerusalem's Temple Mount and the Great Mosque of Cordoba are all testimonies to Umayyad genius.

In Jordan, caravanserais replaced Roman desert fortifications. Hunting lodges, bath houses and "desert castles" soon dotted the desert periphery. Greco-Roman, Byzantine and Sassanid iconography and artistic styles were merged into lavishly decorated walls and floors, paving the way for the development of an idiosyncratic Islamic art. Contrary to Western imagination, the Umayyads appear to have delighted in the representation of human and animal form. The captivating Qusayr Amra on the old trade route from Azraq to Amman, probably patronised by Caliph al-Walid II (743-744) prior to his accession to the throne, displays a wealth of paintings, many of which incorporate artistic idioms from the classically influenced Madaba mosaic school. Dancing girls, bathing beauties and representations of the zodiac vie with images of the "enemies of Islam" and hunting scenes. An extensive palace complex was built on Amman's citadel hill, inclusive of mosque and market place, and a new Islamic Aila prospered near the ancient site on the Gulf of Aqaba until the 11th century.

In 747, a destructive earthquake struck Jordan, an event that probably contributed to the demise of the Umayyad caliphate at the hand of the Abbasids.

This rival family had been plotting a coup for some time from Humayma, an ancient town founded by the Nabataean King Aretas III, located on the trade route between Petra and Aqaba. The Abbasid family chronicles recorded the purchase of the *qarya*, or village, of Humayma by Ali ibn Adballa al-Abbas. During Umayyad Caliph Abed al-Malik ibn Marwan's reign (685-705), a *qasr*

(palace/castel) was built there and 500 olive trees were planted. After his death, his descendant Abu'l Abbas initiated a revolution against the Umayyads, and Humayma ceased to be mentioned in the histories.

Abd ar-Rahman I, grandson of the last truly great Umayyad caliph Hisham (724-43) escaped the Abbasid scourge and made his way to Spain, which was part of the Emirate of Ifriqiya at the time. There he united Al-Andalus, and continued the Umayyad line for another 500 years.

The revolution replacing the Umayyads with the house of Abbas began in the eastern Iranian province of Khurasan and rapidly spread west. The Shia had been simmering with discontent for decades. This opposition was united by an ambitious former Persian slave, Abu Muslim, and fuelled by the claim that succession to the caliphate, which had rightfully been Ali's, had been relinquished by his son Muhammad ibn al Hanafiyya in favour of the descendants of the prophet's uncle Abbas.

The Abbasids (750-969 AD) left their power base in Jordan and moved the capital first to Kufa, Ali's former residence, then to a site near the old Sassanid capital Ctesiphon and designated it Madinat al-Salaam (City of Peace). The name never quite caught on and was soon reverted to that of the original village on the site, Baghdad.

This move away from the multifarious Mediterranean cultural sphere was to have profound influence on the development of Islam. Sassanid bureaucratic structures re-appeared, as did court ritual and culture. Earlier Persian texts were translated into Arabic and Iranian

families who had previously served the Sassanid Shahanshahs were elevated to positions of power within the caliphate. Rigorous interpretation of the book and the law replaced Umayyad flamboyance and magnanimity with a more austere and theocratic political style.

Nonetheless, under Harun al-Rashid (786-809) famously mentioned in the collection of Middle Eastern tales *Thousand and One Nights*, the caliphate experienced a great flowering in culture, a creative period that has subsequently been considered as the Islamic Golden Age. Texts from throughout the Islamic Empire, which by now incorporated a third of the known world, were collected and stored in the *Bayt al-Hikmah*, the "House of Wisdom", a great library and research centre in Baghdad. It gave us the world's most luminous mathematician, Muhammad ibn Musa al-Khwarizmi, whose famous treatise *Aal-jabr wal' muqbla (The Science of Transposition and Cancellation)* formed the basis for modern algebra. Indeed, al-Khwarizmi's very name is found again in the Latin transliteration of the word algorithm. In order to simplify mathematical method, he adopted Hindu numerals and included "zero" into his calculations (later introduced to Europe by Fibonacci). Astronomy, geography, medicine, poetry, philosophy, law – most fields of knowledge today are indebted to the scholars of the *Bayt al-Hikmah*, while the introduction of paper and the building of a paper mill in Baghdad as early as the ninth century facilitated the spread of knowledge.

Although it is generally thought that Jordan declined with the removal of the political centre of the caliphate from Damascus, recent evidence indicates that it continued to enjoy relative prosperity. Churches built during the reign of Harun al-Rashid, attest to

Figurative wall paintings (far left) *decorate the 8th century Umayyad baths complex of Qusayr Amra near the Wadi Butm on the way from Amman to Azraq. Umayyad princes apparently delighted in the depiction of dancing girls, hunting scenes and even of slightly erotic compositions.*

The world-famous heritage site of Qusayr Amra (left) *is undoubtedly the most enchanting of the Umayyad Desert Castles. Extensive paintings decorate the walls of the baths-complex and audience hall. Thought to have been constructed in the mid-8th century by Yazid III, it exemplifies the liberal and internationalist attitude of the first Islamic Caliphate.*

Semi-circular interval towers (right) *with intricate brick work still rise at Qasr Kharana, the Umayyad caravanserai near Wadi Sirhan, a major desert highway linking Arabia and Amman.*

the undisturbed practice of Christianity in Jordan. Further evidence of a close relationship between Jordanian ecclesiastic institutions and Constantinople can be found in the careful removal of human and animal representations from numerous mosaics throughout Jordan in reaction to iconoclast decrees issued by the mother church between the mid-eighth and the mid-ninth centuries. Agriculture too continued to prosper. Grain surpluses in the north now flowed to Baghdad instead of Rome or Constantinople, whilst sugar played an increasingly important role in the Jordan valley's prosperity. Additional income came from catering to Muslim and Christian pilgrims to the Holy Land and to the *Darb al-Hajj*, the pilgrimage route to Mecca.

During this time, maritime trade in the Mediterranean and the Red Sea began to revive and grow at the expense of the overland routes from China to the Mediterranean, affecting many traditional trading communities throughout the peninsula. With the desert castles becoming defunct and the Byzantine and Roman garrisons dismantled, the Transjordanian highlands were open to unchecked migration from the desert. It has been suggested that the "bedouinisation" of Jordan began during this period, when settled agriculturists found it beneficial to enter into tribal or quasi-tribal allegiances with each successive wave of newcomers from the desert.

Conversely, the increase in maritime trade proved beneficial to Egypt, which had access both to the Mediterranean and the Red Sea. It soon became difficult, however, to maintain control over such vast geographical distances from Baghdad. With only tentative central approval, two semi-autonomous states appeared in quick succession. Both were founded by Turkish officers in service of the Abbasid caliph in Baghdad: the Tulunids (868-905) and the Ikhshidids (935-969). Both extended tenuous control over Jordan in a pattern as ancient as time.

For modern Jordanian history, Ikhshidid rule bears special significance. It was considered a duty to maintain the pilgrimage routes to Mecca, and in order to do so they appointed a *sharif* as guardian of the holy sites. King Hussein of the Hijaz, the father of the founder of the Hashemite Kingdom of Jordan King Abdullah I, served as the last Sharif of Mecca, an institution initiated by the Ikhshidids during this period.

While the Abbasids where initially able to control the empire – with the exception of Spain and Morocco – by the end of the ninth century, it began to fragment and a number of local dynasties based on a divergence of religious beliefs appeared. Foremost amongst them were the Ismailis, a secret sect that grew from an argument over

Umayyad villa (far left) *built into the* cavea *of the former Roman theatre at Abila/Qweilbeh.*

Byzantine church at Abila/Qweilbeh (left). *The former Decapolis city was occupied at the same time by Christian Byzantines and Muslim Umayyads.*

the succession to the Sixth Shiite Imam, Jafar al-Sadiq. His eldest son Ismail (hence Ismailis) was passed over in favour of the younger, Musa al-Kazim. Ismail's followers, however recognised the elder as the rightful Seventh Imam, and are, for that reason also called *Sabiya*, or "Seveners", recognising only seven principal Imams after the Prophet's death. Their interpretation of the Holy Koran is fundamentally esoteric and is based on a cyclical view of history centred on the number seven. (The few Ismailis in Jordan today submit to the religious leadership of the Aga Khan). The Ismailis' very active proselytisation of their creed across the region brought about the formation of a number of heretical religious sects.

One such group, the Qaramita, founded a militant tribal republic in eastern Arabia, an event that caused a knock-on effect throughout the peninsula. In the course of this movement, the North Arabian tribal confederation of the Tayy of the House of Jarrah was able to establish itself throughout the Jund of Palestine, wielding nominal power over the region from Ramla until the 11th century. Meanwhile, another Shiite splinter group was able to consolidate power in Tunisia.

Claiming descent from Ali and his wife, the Prophet's daughter Fatima, the Fatimids (969-1171) challenged the Abbasid's political as well as religious authority. In 969, they ousted the Ikhshidids from Egypt, and set up a rival caliphate in Cairo in 973. From there they extended their influence along the entire North African coast including Morocco with astonishing speed, then moved north along the age-old invasion route of the Levantine littoral taking Palestine,

Jordan and most of Syria. In 977, the Jarrah at Ramla began paying tribute to the Fatimids.

Under the Fatimid anti-Caliph al-Hakim (996-1012) the destruction of 30,000 churches and Christian shrines was carried out in Jordan and Syria as well as in Egypt and Palestine, including that of the Church of the Holy Sepulchre in Jerusalem. This act was to become a contributing factor to the declaration of what was seen as a holy war against the Muslim "heathen" by Pope Urban II, as it was an act eminently suited to incite religious fervour and thus political support for the Crusades.

Al-Hakim declared himself a divine representation of God and endeavoured to have his own name replace that of Allah in inscriptions and during prayer services. This, and decrees such as banning the yearly *Hajj* to Mecca and fasting during Ramadan, finally culminated in a schism at the Fatimid court. In 1021, al-Hakim appears to have been discreetly assassinated. His most loyal followers, however, preferred to interpret his disappearance as an act of divine concealment (*ghayba*) and opted to wait for his return as *Mahdi*. One of his closest disciples, Mohammed ibn Ismail al-Darazi, left Cairo and began preaching the new faith in Syria. The Druze (from an anglicised version of *durzi*), a religious sect still found in Israel, Lebanon, Syria and Jordan, are descended from this fervent missionary.

While the Fatimids were challenging Abbasid rule from the southwest, the Seljuks, a Turkish tribe from the Aral Sea region, were infiltrating the caliphate from the east. Although the Abbasids ostensibly

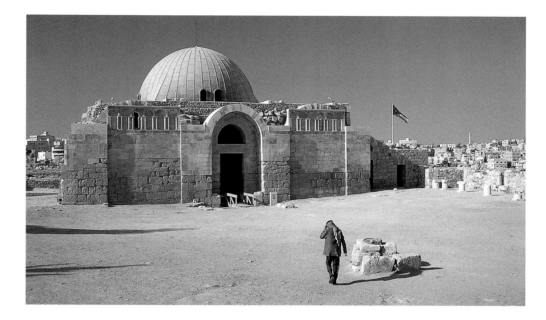

Eighth century Umayyad palace complex (right) *with reconstructed dome on Citadel Hill, overlooking Amman.*

continued to rule the Islamic east, by 1058 the Seljuks had effectively usurped Abbasid power in Baghdad and established a capital at Isfahan in Iran. From there, they organised a formidable army and pushed west towards the shrunken Byzantine Empire. As orthodox Sunni Muslims, their ultimate goal was to vanquish the heretical Fatimids.

In 1071 the Seljuk Sultan Alp Arsalan (1063-1072) won a decisive battle against the Byzantines at Manzikert, capturing the Emperor Romanus Diogenes (1068-1071). After this humiliation Romanus seems to have abdicated and retired to a monastery, while Arsalan returned triumphantly in possession of Jerusalem, Edessa, Antioch, Hieropolis and the emperor's daughter as a bride for his son and successor Malikshah (1072-1092). Malikshah became Sultan of Isfahan the following year.

Despite the Great Schism that had formally divided the Christian Church in 1054, the bedraggled Byzantine leadership saw no alternative but to send pleas for help to the western papacy.

In the wake of the Seljuk-Byzantine war, Turkish mercenaries began infiltrating Syria and Jordan, paving the way for a formal invasion in 1086. The Fatimids withdrew from the region, but managed to reoccupy some of the Palestinian coastal cities in 1089. Meanwhile, the Seljuks had established the Sultanate of Rum in the former Byzantine territory of Anatolia and set up an administrative centre in Aleppo, governed by Malikshah's brother, Tutush. Upon Tutush' death, Syria was divided between his sons Duqaq and Ridwan. Ridwan was by all accounts a terrifying young man (strongly influenced by a "physician-astrologer" from the putative Assassin sect, a militant offshoot of the Fatimid Ismailis), who set

about eliminating his rivals. To escape his brother's bloodthirsty politics Duqaq fled to Damascus and was promptly proclaimed sultan of that city.

At the close of the 11th century Jordan fell under the jurisdiction of the Damascene kingdom of Duqaq, though how much control was exercised is open to debate. Infighting between disparate groups was rife. Turkish freebooters, Bedouin brigands and Fatimid armies desperate to reoccupy parts of their former empire were taking their toll on the local population. Pilgrimage to Muslim, Christian and Jewish holy sites had become all but impossible.

In one last effort, the Fatimids regained control of Jerusalem in 1098, taking advantage of the Turkish preoccupation with the arrival of the Franks. Jerusalem had by this time become the "third most holy place of God" for Islam. For this was the place where the Trumpets of Resurrection would sound for all of mankind to assemble in the valley of Gehenna outside the eastern city wall of Jerusalem, to be judged by God. Many of the Muslim mystics who had made their home in Jerusalem had been preaching the coming of an apocalypse, a message that seemed wholly justified with the arrival of the First Crusade.

Duqaq's fears of assassination were confirmed when he was duly poisoned and the rule of Damascus and its dependencies fell to his tutor, the *Atabeg* Tughtigin, a lame former slave with high political ambitions. His descendants ruled the region in form of the Burid Atabegs until 1154.

On the eve of invasion by the crusaders, the Seljuk realm was fragmented. Every city seemed to have a different ruler who, more

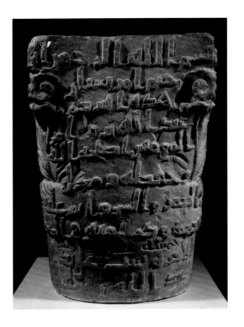

Decorative capital and water gauge from the Umayyad reservoir at Muwaqqar built by Caliph Yazid II. The calligraphy relief of simple Kufic letters mentions the date 723 and incorporates several water level marks.

often than not, was divorced from the influence of Isfahan and locked in dispute with their neighbours. As much as one could speak of any unity, their enmity and military strategy was directed towards the Fatimids. For the crusaders, this political and military fragmentation proved to be a decisive advantage.

On the 27th of November 1095, an assembly of clergy, knights and common men stood freezing in a field in Clermont, France, listening to a passionate sermon by Pope Urban II. He called for a holy war to free the Christians of the East from what he saw as the yoke of Muslim oppression, and liberate the Church of the Holy Sepulchre in Jerusalem. In return, he promised salvation and eternal life in heaven. The popular response was unequivocal and electric.

In the spring of the following year, the so-called Peasant Crusade, an unorganised posse of adventurers under the leadership of the fanatical hermit Peter Amiens, left France only to be annihilated by the Turks in Anatolia. At the same time, the leaders of the First Crusade, among them Robert of Normandy, Godfrey of Boullion, Baldwin of Flanders, Raymond of Toulouse, Bohemond of Tarentum and his nephew Tancred, left Europe for the Holy Land. After a victory against the Sultan of Rum and a long drawn-out siege of Antioch, they marched down the Mediterranean coast and stormed Jerusalem on the 15th of July 1099. The invasion amounted to a massacre. Ibn al-Athir, the Arab chronicler of the time wrote: "*the population of the holy city was put to the sword, and the Franjj spent a week massacring Muslims*".

As a consequence of their victories, three Crusader states were established to include the whole of Palestine and the Syrian coast all the way to Anatolia, divided amongst the principal leaders of the campaign. The Kingdom of Jerusalem went to Godfrey of Boullion; Antioch to Bohemond; and Edessa to his brother Baldwin. The land from the northern shore of the Dead Sea, along the King's Highway to the Gulf of Aqaba, was incorporated into the Kingdom of Jerusalem. It became one of 16 feudal fiefs with the official designation of *Oultre Jourdain* (Transjordan) also called the Seigneury of Crac (Karak) and Montreal (Shobak). The highlands to the north of Amman and the fertile grain-growing region remained as part of the Burid Atabegate, still ruled by Tughtigin the Lame, now a fervent enemy of the crusaders.

The settlement and organisation of the newly conquered lands was a slow process. The native population was of mixed origin with a variety of divergent religious and tribal allegiances. Furthermore, the brutal repression that marked early crusader policy had not endeared the new overlords to the locals. Godfrey's successor, King Baldwin I, crossed the Jordan River and personally took control of the King's Highway. A series of castles and military garrisons were built to form a line of defence from Turkey to Aqaba, each a day's ride from the next. The impressive Shobak castle was established in 1115, followed by fortifications in Aqaba and on the Isle de Gray just off the coast. Another was built at Wueira near Petra and a further stronghold in Petra itself. Finally in 1140, construction work was begun at Karak, a site as old as Moab. Crac/Karak became the administrative centre of the region, controlling agriculture as well as salt production from the Red Sea.

Inscribed stone slab in the 'Cave of the Seven Sleepers' near Amman, one of the sites connected to the legend of seven youths saved from persecution by falling asleep in a cave for centuries. It is common to both Christian and Islamic traditions.

The crusaders had come to stay, and while a large number of soldiers went home after the first victories, they were soon replaced by a steady trickle of European settlers. With the seemingly impenetrable high castles of Shobak and Karak as the nuclei for the defence of the Latin eastern front, Jordan had re-emerged in its age old role as a multiethnic buffer state between opposing powers. The King's Highway once again facilitated the large movement of troops, pilgrims and merchandise, bringing much needed revenue to the region.

Whilst the crusaders held Jordan from Amman to the Dead Sea, the north continued to be controlled by Damascus. There, the new dynasty of the Zengids was on the rise and campaigned vigorously against the European invaders. Zengi, the former governor of Mosul and veteran of the crusader battle of Aleppo in 1124, took the city by force four years later and made it the centre of resistance against the Latin armies. His son Nur-al-Din (1145-74) wrested Edessa from the heirs of Baldwin, providing the catalyst for the Second Crusade. In late April 1154, through persuasion rather than by force, it was reported at the time, Nur al-Din entered Damascus, inaugurating its most prosperous period in centuries.

As the ruler of a united Aleppo and Damascus and their hinterlands, Nur al-Din pursued a policy of solidarity among the disparate Turkish statelets, and of vicious resistance to the European invaders. Uniting them by his military prowess as much as by his powerful personality, he called for a *jihad* or Holy War against the enemies of Islam. Unlike the despotic Turkish rulers preceding him, he abandoned the royal robes in favour of simple clothing. Tall and

dark, clean shaven but for a goatee, he cultivated an image of piety and justice, setting a precedent for a new type of Islamic ruler. By 1157 he had organised an army and was ready for direct confrontation with the *Franjj* – as they are referred to in Arab chronicles – in Jerusalem. He may well have succeeded had not an earthquake of catastrophic proportions struck the whole of Syria. His dream was left to be realised by one of the most colourful personalities of the Crusader period, Salah ud-Din Yussuf ibn Ayyub (1169-93), better known to Western historians as Saladin.

Born of Kurdish ancestry in Tikrit (present day Iraq), Saladin had entered the service of Nur al-Din, and was promptly sent with his uncle Shirkuh on the Egyptian campaign of 1169. As vizier, he transformed Egypt into an Ayyubid power base. In 1171, he deposed the young Fatimid ruler and re-established Sunni orthodoxy. Sensing the advent of a new political rival, Nur al-Din accused Saladin of mutiny. In one of many acts that shaped Saladin's reputation as the epitome of the wise and magnanimous Islamic ruler, he avoided conflict with Damascus. Instead, he focused on revitalising Egypt's economy and on extending his influence to the Hijaz and Yemen. Only after Nur al-Din's death in 1174, did he move his forces north and marched into Damascus and Aleppo, subsequently uniting Sunni leaders behind him and against a common enemy, the Franks.

The following year an attempt was made on Saladin's life. The culprit was known – and feared – throughout the Islamic world: Sinan ibn Salman ibn Muhammad, also known as Rashid al-Din, the head of the militant Ismaili Assassin sect of Syria, who had threatened Saladin years earlier. The Assassins were founded by Hassan-i

Sabba, "the old man of the mountain" and master of Alamut, a fanatically anti-Seljuk stronghold located deep in the Elborz mountains, north of present day Teheran. Not unlike modern terrorists, they targeted religious and political leaders as a means of extending their influence through fear and intimidation, buttressed by a fanatical following, willing to die for their master and his cause.

Rashid al-Din had never forgiven Saladin for disposing the Fatimids. The first attempt on Saladin's life was followed by a second one in 1176, which left him visibly shaken. Although he initiated a siege on Masyaf, the Assassin's Syrian stronghold, Saladin suddenly withdrew for unexplained reasons. An agreement must have been reached, though historic sources diverge on his true reasons for disengagement. The Assassins continued as a substantial political force in the Near East until the Mongol invasion. Thus in the latter part of the 12th century, three religio-political groups faced off against another: Christian crusaders, Sunni orthodoxy and Shiite militants. By reasons of its geographical position, Jordan once more became the location for bitter rivalry.

Shortly after his marriage to the heiress of Karak castle in 1177, the former prince of Antioch Reynald de Chatillon, victoriously engaged Saladin at the battle of Montgisart. History has often juxtaposed his notoriously ambitious and cruel acts to Saladin's much praised chivalry. Flagrantly ignoring a truce called between Saladin and the leper king of Jerusalem Baldwin IV, de Chatillon continued to raid caravan trains and shipping in the Red Sea. In November 1183, Ayyubid siege engines began to bombard the fortress of Karak in retaliation. A much told and often embellished story has Saladin find

a wedding in progress, prompting him to direct his assault away from the marriage chamber. The siege of Karak was unsuccessful, leaving de Chatillon to his favourite pastime of targeting pilgrims on their *hajj* to Mecca. In response, Ajlun castle was built by Saladin's cousin Izz ad-Din Usama, on the site of the ancient Raepta in the hill country north of Jarash, thus securing the northern routes. Today, it stands as an impressive and rare example of Islamic military architecture.

It took Saladin another four years to consolidate the strength of his army. The decisive battle of Hattin near Lake Tiberias, fought in the heat of high summer on the 4th of July 1187, turned fortune in his favour. Saladin personally beheaded de Chatillon, and, one by one, the occupied cities of Palestine and the Levant fell to him. After three months, he had taken Jerusalem and restored it to Muslim jurisdiction. Meanwhile, a Third Crusade had arrived, reinforcing Christian control of the Palestinian coast. With the Peace of Ramallah, an armistice was agreed with Richard the Lionheart of England, defining the coast as Christian lands while Jerusalem remained under Muslim control, with rights of passage granted to Christian pilgrims.

Jordan, especially in the south, had served as a principal buffer zone, providing military bases for campaigns fought against Muslim armies. Trade increased somewhat during the Latin occupation, but had never again reached its former potential. By the end of the twelfth century, commerce with China and India had become almost wholly restricted to maritime routes, whilst goods from Persia and beyond arrived in Syria via the northern overland routes with their termini at Aleppo and Damascus, without reaching the Transjordanian nexi. Jordan simply fell out of the system.

Although the Crusades did not achieve lasting results in terms of military conquest, their long term influence on Western society was incalculable. The eastern Mediterranean was opened to European shipping, whilst Venetians and Genoese established trading colonies in Egypt through which Eastern luxury goods found their way to European markets. As early as 1082, they had been granted the right to trade throughout Byzantium without paying customs duties. For the history of the Middle Ages, this proved a far more important factor than ephemeral conquests. Eastern fashions, architecture, art and learning infused a culturally stagnant Western Europe with new stimuli, ultimately paving the way for the European Renaissance. Commercial and political intervention in Eastern trade was to become a constant recurring theme throughout the following centuries, eventually leading to widespread colonial control of the region in the 19th century.

The Later Islamic Era

The dawn of the 13th century saw the amalgamation of a great pagan power in the steppes of Central Asia. United by Ghengis Khan, the Mongol confederation of nomadic horsemen laid waste to the Ch'in Empire and with terrifying speed moved west into Muslim territory. By 1220 the great cities of Samarkand and Bukhara were in their hands. Merv and Nishapur along with the east of Iran soon followed. After the death of Ghengis Khan, the empire was partitioned between four of his sons, who maintained a permanent central capital at Karakoram, the fabled city between Mongolia and the Great Wall of China. From here, they set out to subjugate all who lived beneath the four directions of the sky.

While Kublai Khan initiated his campaign to encircle and subsequently divide the Sung Empire of China, Hulagu drove his cavalry west with the intention of conquering the Muslim world between the Oxus River and the Nile. One by one, Armenia, Georgia and northern Mesopotamia fell to his horsemen. The Turkish principalities of Anatolia fared no better, and even the unassailable Assassin strongholds failed to resist the mounted warriors from the steppes. In February 1258, the Mongol hordes laid waste to Baghdad, destroying its religious and academic institutions and bringing the long reign of the Abbasid caliphs to an end. Seemingly unstoppable, Hulagu accomplished the overthrow of Aleppo and Damascus the following year, and rapidly encroached on Jordan and Palestine. He never got to take Egypt. In September 1260, at the battle of Ain Jalut (the spring of Goliath) near Nazareth in Palestine, his army was utterly defeated by Baybars and his *mamluke* soldier-slaves.

Baybars, a Turkish military slave from the northern shores of the Black Sea, had risen to power in the dying days of the Ayyubids in Egypt. The last viable Ayyubid sultan of Cairo was killed during the Sixth Crusade of King Louis IX of France in 1250, leaving a power vacuum to be only partially filled by his concubine Shajar al-Durr. A female sultan was unheard of in the history of Islam, and the politically fragmented principalities unanimously protested against her accession to the throne of Egypt. Shortly after his victory over the Mongols, Baybars assumed the title of sultan and united Egypt and Syria. Then he turned his military genius to expelling the crusaders from the coastline of Palestine.

The Mamluke Dynasty (1260-1516) was to rule Jordan until the beginning of the 16th century. Once again the frontier was defined on the line Euphrates-Aqaba, with Jordan serving as the border between the Mongols in the east and the Mamlukes of Syria and Egypt. Baybars divided his realm into six provinces called *mamalik*. Jordan came under the wider rule of Damascus, though it effectively remained an outpost of the empire. In time, Ajlun, Saladin's castle in the olive growing region north of Jarash was renovated and became the administrative centre of the north, while Karak, the imposing crusader fortress, served in the same capacity for the south. During this time of uneasy peace, pilgrims once more moved freely along the King's Highway. Irrigation systems were rebuilt and sugar production became a major industry, both for regional and international markets.

The sweet cane had spread from the South Sea Islands to India and Persia a thousand years before it was discovered there by the invading Muslim armies. From the eighth century onward the art

Pottery from the Mamluke period of types common throughout Jordan and Syria between the 13th and 15th centuries.

of refining the reed had been adopted by the Arab world. Sugar subsequently became an important luxury and export item and sold at the equivalent of £50 a kilo in 14th century London. Remnants of a Mamluke sugar refinery still survive at Tawaheen as-Sukkar near the town of as-Safi south of the Dead Sea, its very name redolent of a once thriving industry. Other sugar factories have been found at Mazra'a and Feifeh, and further up the Jordan valley.

Mongol hegemony from China to the Euphrates initiated a new golden age of trade. For the first time in the history of the Silk Road, merchants were able to travel from the Mediterranean all the way to China, a journey well documented by the Venetian traveller, trader and adventurer Marco Polo. As is often the case in history, this *Pax Mongolia* was short lived. By 1380, a new Turko-Mongol tribal confederation under the leadership of Tamerlane, blazed through the Middle East. Central Asia, India, Iran and Syria collapsed under its thundering impact. The great city of Damascus was sacked in 1400-1, initiating a political and economic decline throughout the region. The new overlords destroyed the remaining repositories of ancient knowledge and killed or deported scholars and scientist, generating a cultural recession of devastating proportions. For the Muslim East, the second Mongol invasion proved disastrous.

Already weakened by internal pressures, it never fully regained it previous power.

By the 15th century, Jordan had been reduced to a few forti-fied towns and a handful of agricultural villages. The great cities of Amman, Jarash, Pella and Gadara were gone. Increased migration from the desert was "bedounising" the south, whilst a tribal emirate of local peasants known as the Ghzawis rose in the north. Like many of the surviving local families, they claimed Bedouin descent and formed intricate tribal allegiances. From Ajlun they were able to extend their influence across the Jordan River to agricultural areas around Hebron and Jerusalem. In 1516, Jordan was annexed to the Ottoman Empire; its fortunes, however, changed little.

The Ottoman state was born on the frontier between the Islamic world and the remnants of the Byzantine Empire. Nomads driven from the steppes of Turkestan by the Mongol expansion had moved west into Anatolia and the former Seljuk principalities. By the 14th century they had united under their first ruler Uthman (hence Ottoman) and were pushing west into Christian lands. In 1354 they crossed the Dardanelles and headed for Gallipoli and Adrianople. Significantly, the same year saw the first signing of an Ottoman-Genoese commercial treaty. Their fourth ruler Bayezid I (1380-1401) incorporated all of Anatolia and revived the old Seljuk title "Sultan of Rum".

Tamerlane's military campaigns did little to halt Ottoman expansion. On the 29th of May 1453 Mehmed II took up residence in the former Byzantine capital, Constantinople, and the fledgling

Ajlun Castle north of Jarash was build by Saladin's cousin Izz ad-Din Usama in 1184-5. It is a rare example of Islamic military architecture and was constructed as a counterpart to the Crusader castle of Belvoir just across the Jordan river. Later it became an administrative centre under the famous Mamluke Sultan Baybars, who added the south-west tower.

sultanate emerged as a powerful new Islamic empire. Firearms imported from the West facilitated further military expansion, and, by the early 16th century the Ottomans had established hegemony from Anatolia to Egypt and North Africa, down both shores of the Read Sea, Arabia and Iraq. The Ottoman fleet soon dominated the Mediterranean, the Red Sea and the Indian Ocean. In 1529 Suleyman the Magnificent (1520-1566), better known to Turkish history as Suleyman the Lawgiver, even advanced across Hungary and besieged Vienna.

Ottoman domains were divided into provinces, presided over by local governors or Pashas. Jordan's two main administrative centres of Karak and Ajlun survived in their previous roles, whilst the Ghzawi family, who had already exerted considerable power during the Mamlukes, now collected taxes on behalf of Istanbul instead of Cairo. The Ghzawis were also awarded the lucrative office of *Amir al-Hajj*, leaders and protectors of the pilgrim caravan from Damascus to the holy city of Mecca, for which a budget of 100,000 gold sovereigns was allocated by the Sublime Porte in Istanbul. A large part of this budget went to bribe the ever-proliferating tribal chiefs along the way. To augment the security of the yearly procession and to ensure the necessary water supply, the Ottomans built a chain of Hajj-forts along the desert caravan route (Mafraq, Zarqa, Belqa, Qatrana, Heza, Aneza and Ma'an), thus sidelining the old King's Highway. Another pilgrim fort was maintained in Aqaba, catering to the *Dharb al-Hajj* from Cairo.

During the first three centuries of Ottoman hegemony, Transjordan subsisted as a neglected backwater where Ottoman control was negligible and the region was open to a steady flow of migrants from the Arabian Peninsula. North Arabian Adwan tribes, Anaza Bedouins from central Arabia, and later the Huwaytat tribes laid claim to the desert periphery from Aqaba to Ajlun, impinging on the surviving agricultural lands.

Whilst Suleyman the Magnificent was still adding new territories to his vast domain, another revolution was under way in Europe. The construction of better, faster ships and the discovery of new sea routes threatened to sideline the eastern Mediterranean ports. The colonisation of the Americas, the coastal river deltas of Africa and former Arab trading posts in south and south-east Asia began to undermine Muslim monopolies. Soon, cheap Western imports were competing with Eastern goods and, by the 17th century, sugar from the West Indies was refined in Marseilles, France, and bought by merchants in Istanbul, causing widespread inflation throughout the empire. A second siege of Vienna in 1683 ended with Ottoman defeat and the signing of the treaty of Karlowitz – a treaty that signalled a marked shift in the balance of power between East and West. As a result, Austria began pushing into the Balkans, Russia threatened to intrude from the north and east, while Portuguese, Dutch and British maritime superiority was weakening Ottoman trade connections. It was during these setbacks for the Ottoman Near East that France entered the power game. In 1798, General Napoleon Bonaparte occupied Egypt and quickly attempted to move up the Levantine littoral into Palestine. The incursion failed and French troops withdrew from the region.

At the same time, Wahhabiism, a new movement founded by a

A 13th or 14th century minaret still calls the faithful to prayer in the old mosque in Ajlun town. Today, Ajlun supports a large Christian community.

militant theologian in the Najd region of central Arabia, was gaining followers. Muhammad ibn Abd al-Wahhab (1703-1783) preached a return to an authentic Islam as set out by the Prophet and the word of God while advocating a strict interpretation of Islamic law. This was a direct challenge to Ottoman authority. Amongst his converts was Muhammad ibn Saud, then the governor of the small market town. At the turn of the 19th century, the Wahhabis burst out from the desert and attacked the Shia cities of Karbala and Najaf, then turned their attention west to the holy cities of all Muslims, Mecca and Medina. The *jihad* was carried north towards Jordan, where the new sect had already found avid supporters amongst the Anaza Bedouins. By order of Istanbul, this rebellion was put down by the Ottoman governor of Egypt, Muhammad Ali Pasha in seven years of fighting between 1811 and 1818. Ejected from the Hijaz but far from beaten, the Wahhabis moved east. The Ottoman Empire was in decay.

Throughout the 19th century European involvement in the Middle East grew on all fronts. European steamship services and newly constructed railroads facilitated the transport of goods and armies, while British, French, German and Italian banks dominated the money economy. In 1830 France annexed Algeria, a year later Britain colonised the port of Aden, whilst Russia continued to penetrate Ottoman and Iranian territory. The Crimean war saw a temporary shift in allegiances, with France and Britain fighting side by side with Ottoman soldiers against Russia. But the truce was short-lived.

The opening of the Suez Canal in 1869 finally provided European shipping with a direct route to India. Within two decades Britain, by now the most powerful European sea-power and in control of the most important global trade routes, occupied Egypt ostensibly to protect the Suez nexus.

Then a new powerful player entered the Great Game. The unification of Germany in 1871 had brought on a technical revolution of unprecedented dimensions there. Within a decade, German engineers, bankers and military personnel flooded into Istanbul, proposing projects of gargantuan dimensions. A railroad was to connect Berlin with Baghdad and ultimately the port of Basra. In British political circles at the time, this proposed new overland trade route was interpreted as a blatant challenge to British trade superiority. Construction began in 1888 and eight years later it was possible to travel by rail from Berlin all the way to Konya deep in the heartland of Anatolia. The Hijaz Railway became part of the greater German transport projects.

On the day of the 25th anniversary of his accession to the Ottoman throne, Sultan Abdul Hamid II inaugurated the construction of a new railway line which was to connect Damascus with Islam's holiest city, Mecca. Financed by collections around the Muslim world, the route roughly followed the *Darb al-Hajj* through Jordan via Amman and Ma'an from whence it turned south-east into the Hijaz. In 1908 the railroad tracks had reached Medina, when the military coup of the Young Turks in Istanbul put a halt to the endeavour. It was never completed, but parts of its tracks are still in use for the transport of phosphates from el-Hesa to Aqaba today.

Whilst the Industrial Revolution had catapulted Europe into the forefront of world economic supremacy, the stakes were raised further by the discovery of petroleum. This fungible product has

Qatrana Hajj fort on the Desert Highway near the turn-off to the King's Highway and Karak. Constructed in the time of the Ottoman ruler Suleyman the Magnificent (1520-66), Qatrana is typical of a chain of castles built to protect pilgrims on their way to the holy city of Mecca. In the early 20th century, many of these caravanserais became stops along the Hijaz Railway Line.

dominated global economics and politics ever since. Kerosene was first used in lamps developed by the German inventor Stohwasser in 1853. By 1870, Russian steamships in the Caspian were already powered by a heavy oil they called "Masut". The same year the American financier J. D. Rockefeller founded the Standard Oil Company. In 1882, the year that Britain occupied Egypt, Captain (later Admiral) Fisher lobbied forcefully for the overhaul of the British fleet and the conversion from coal to oil. Within months of Fisher's appeal to parliament, the German engineer Gottlieb Daimler had developed the first petrol motor and powered his daughter's toy car with it.

During the last decade of the 19th century the maverick explorer and geologist William D'Arcy, ostensibly searching for the secrets of Zoroastrian fire temples, was criss-crossing the Iranian desert. In exchange for $20,000 and a promise of a 16% cut of the profits, he received a 60 year concession from the Persian Qajar Shah Mozsaffaru'd-Din, granting him and his heirs the right to dig and drill Iranian soil. The year was 1901. On his way to Paris to sign a contract with the banking house of Rothschild to finance his project, he was intercepted by the British superspy of the time, S.G. Rosenblum, also known as Sidney Reilly, who convinced him to sign with the newly established Anglo-Persian oil company instead. Thus, Britain gained its most lucrative oil concession in the Middle East.

In 1909, the first oil-powered war ships left German harbours. In response, Winston Churchill in his capacity as Navy minister, initiated the overhaul of the British fleet. In 1912, in the course of negotiations concerning the Berlin-Baghdad railway, Germany secured the

mineral rights to the soil parallel to the tracks, which by now extended as far as Mosul in northern Iraq. The following year, the British government acquired the majority of the Anglo-Persian oil shares, to be renamed later British Petroleum (BP). In 1914, the "war to end all wars" was declared, leading to the collapse of the old order in the Near and Middle East.

In the preceding decades of decline in the Ottoman Empire, a sense of nationalism had begun to take root in the increasingly westernised upper echelons of Istanbul society, eventually giving rise to the Young Turks and the military coup of 1908, terminating seven centuries of continuous rule by the Ottoman Dynasty. German trained Turkish army officers ruled an autocratic state, designed to centralise power and tighten control over its dominions. When World War I broke out, the Turks entered on the side of Germany against Britain, France and Russia. At the same time, influenced by the rapid "turkification" of the empire, pan-Arab movements began to make themselves felt across the region. The first voices were heard amongst the educated Arabs residing in Istanbul, in Syria and Iraq. Later, these voices found a leader in the protector of the holy cities of Islam, the Sharif of Mecca and Medina, Hussein ibn Ali.

Although Britain had by all accounts long kept contact with pan-Arab groups, when World War I broke out these political manoeuvres reached fever pitch. At the height of the Great War in 1916, an Arab Revolt was declared against what was nominally still Ottoman rule. Many legends have since clouded the sequence of events leading to the revolt, most notable of which have been the romanticised narratives of Colonel T.E. Lawrence in his *Seven Pillars*

of Wisdom. It is generally agreed, however, that the principal impetus was provided by correspondence between the British High Commissioner of Egypt, Sir Henry McMahon, and the sharifian household, promising the establishment of a future pan-Arab state. Sharif Hussein was thus acclaimed King of the Arabs.

Unbeknownst to the Arab nationalists, however, an Anglo-French agreement was signed (Sykes-Picot) in the same year and ratified by Italy and Czarist Russia, carving up the Ottoman Empire between them. Greater Syria and the oil-reserves of the Mosul region (the German concessions) were to go to France, whilst Britain would inherit Jordan and Palestine with the strategic ports of Haifa and Acre, and central and southern Iraq with the cities of Baghdad and Basra. It also included permission to connect Haifa and Baghdad via future French territory. Italy was allocated the mountain region along the coast of southern Anatolia and the islands off-shore, whilst Russia was promised Armenia and parts of Kurdistan.

A year later, while the Sharif's third son Feisal was fighting Turkish forces in Transjordan, a letter of far reaching implications was exchanged between the British Foreign Secretary Arthur Balfour and Walter Lord Rothschild, avid supporter of the international Zionist movement. It declared His Majesty's support for the establishment of a homeland for the Jewish people in Palestine, and decreed that *"nothing shall be done which may prejudice the civil and religious rights of existing non-Jewish communities"*. These same non-Jewish communities amounted to over 85% of the population at the time in 1917.

On the 1st October 1918 Feisal and Lawrence entered Damascus, where Feisal immediately established himself at the head of an Arab government, acknowledging his father's ultimate suzerainty as King of the Arabs. With the Mudros armistice hostilities were brought to an end and the Ottoman Empire ceased to exist. At the end of the war, Britain was in control of Palestine, France exerted power over the northern coastal areas, whilst Feisal was consolidating Greater Syria, which included Jordan, Syria and parts of Lebanon. For the time being, however, all of the occupied former enemy territories, as they were referred to, remained under the overall control of the British General Edmund Allenby.

Within months of Feisal's arrival in Damascus, French forces landed in Beirut, laying claim to Syria. The situation was brought to a head during the peace negotiations in Versailles in 1919, where Feisal called for a commission to investigate Syrian unity. The subsequently appointed King-Crane commission duly reported the strong Arab opposition to the proposed mandates and, more significantly, it advised against unchecked Jewish immigration to Palestine. The report was not made public until 1922, two years after the San Remo Conference during which the Balfour Declaration was reaffirmed. It also called for an "appropriate Jewish agency" to aid in the establishment of a Jewish homeland in Palestine. Contrary to recommendations, the British experiment envisaging a peaceful coexistence of Jews and Palestinians under British administration went ahead.

A month after Feisal had been proclaimed head of an independent Arab kingdom of Syria by the General Syrian Congress in Damascus, Palestine and Transjordan came under the rule of the British Mandate, whilst Syria and Lebanon were ceded to the French.

Reliefs of a coffee grinder on a local Sheik's tomb in Qastal. The grinder, or mihbash, symbolises generosity, and signifies the importance of the dignitary entombed. The real mihbash is made from the wood of the wild pistachio tree.

Essentially, this put into effect a large part of the Sykes-Picot agreement. During the same congressional meeting, Feisal's elder brother Abdullah was offered the crown of Iraq. In July 1920, the new French high commissioner in Beirut sent troops to occupy Damascus. King Feisal left Damascus to, ultimately, establish a new government in Iraq.

In the waning light of its empire, Ottoman rule had tightened its control over Jordan. The country was divided into three regions, adding the *kaza* of al-Balqa to the two established administrative centres of Ajlun and Karak, whilst the seaport of Aqaba was attached to the district of Medina in the Hijaz. Military garrisons were revived, partially to enforce new land and tax reforms and partially to control the Bedouin tribal chiefs. Whilst the reforms were not popular, they did bring renewed stability to Transjordan; some of the abandoned towns were resettled, whilst others, such as Madaba grew in size. This process was aided significantly by the immigration of Circassian farmers from the Caucasus who had fled Russian persecution after the Crimean war.

Opposition to the new policies generated two minor revolts in the first decade of the 20th century in the former crusader towns of Shobak and Karak, followed by an up-rising of the Druze in the Hauran district. A census to determine the availability of young men for conscription to the Ottoman military service brought about an eight day revolt in Karak, Tafila and Ma'an, resulting in the arrest and execution of the ringleaders. A general amnesty in 1912 re-established the status quo and relative stability.

When the Great Arab Revolt was proclaimed by Sharif Hussein of Mecca, Transjordan became a battlefield. In command of an army of regular and irregular soldiers, Amir Feisal conducted a valiant guerrilla war from bases in the desert between Azraq and Aqaba. His military tactics effectively interrupted Ottoman communications and troop transports, paving the way for his victorious entry into Damascus.

After the war, Jordan fell under the jurisdiction of Feisal's short-lived government in Damascus. In 1919, it was distributed amongst three administrative regions, with only the central area of the Balqa – which included Salt, Amman (reoccupied by the Circassians) and Madaba – wholly on Jordanian land. The north, with its centre at Ajlun became part of the Syrian Hauran, whilst the south extended into the Hijaz, each ruled by a sharifian tribal council. After Feisal's flight from Damascus in 1920, many of his political supporters found refuge in Transjordan, a region then rapidly falling into anarchy.

On the 11th of November 1920, Abdullah, second son and former foreign minister of King Hussein of the Hijaz, arrived by train from Medina in the sleepy border oasis of Ma'an. Equipped with little more than a handful of men, political tenacity tempered by pragmatism and a dream to reclaim the "Arab Nation of Greater Syria", he set about shaping the future of the land that was to become the Hashemite Kingdom of Jordan a quarter of a century later.

Although part of their Palestinian mandate, British control over Transjordan was weak. No less than three regional governments were recognised, each headed by a special advisor reporting to Jerusalem. In the north the government of Ajlun now resided at

The former Ottoman administrative centre of Salt (far left), *north west of Amman, still retains a large number of exquisite late-Ottoman town houses.*

The house of the Bisharat family (left) *in Amman reflects late Ottoman urban design, typical of eastern Mediterranean architecture of that period.*

Decorative entrance (right) *to a late-Ottoman town house in Salt.*

Irbid, the central territory had its seat at Salt, and the south, a troublesome land with the grandiose name of the Arab Government of Moab, was once more administered from Karak. Only the central region, settled largely by the Circassians of Amman, the Christians of Salt and Madaba and including some Palestinian families from Nablus and Nazareth, resembled a functioning local government. Both, Ajlun and Moab continued to be riddled by uprisings and inter-tribal squabbles. Together, however, they formed the very heart of the historic land between Syria and the Red Sea.

Abdullah left Ma'an in February 1921 to amalgamate the thus far "unallocated" territory of Transjordan, and to establish a base in Amman. A month later, the British colonial secretary Winston Churchill called a conference of leading "orientalists" in Cairo to decide the future of the Middle East. Familiar names, such as T.E. Lawrence, Sir Percy Cox and Gertrude Bell were on the guest list. Abdullah was encouraged to renounce his claim to the Syrian project and the Iraqi throne in exchange for Transjordan east of the Jordan River. Feisal was duly placed on the throne in Baghdad, his fledgling government aided by the British airforce, his administration run for the time being by the Anglo-Persian oil company. In 1922 the League of Nations ruled in favour of the establishment of an independent Emirate of Transjordan separate from the British Mandate, a ruling that became effective on the 15th of May 1923.

While the British continued to control Palestine directly, partially in the moral fulfilment of the Balfour declaration, Transjordan was represented by a series of advisors reporting to the High Commission in Jerusalem. By all accounts, the relationship between the Emir's new government and his British advisors was more often than not strained, while disappointed Arab nationalists protested vocally against his acceptance of British political fiat. As part of the constitutional agreements, a small Transjordanian army was organised by F.G. Peake, mainly to suppress tribal squabbles and to repel Wahhabi raids. This force was later to grow into the Arab Legion, headed by a long-serving British Lieutenant-General, Sir John Bagot Glubb, better known as "Glubb Pasha".

By the beginning of World War I, the House of Saud had extended its influence over most of eastern Arabia. In 1924, Wahhabi forces moved once more into the Hijaz, a region still under the rule of King Hussein. This time there was no help, and the hero of the Arab Revolt was forced to abdicate in favour of his eldest son Ali and to flee to Aqaba. Within a year, Ibn Saud had occupied the holy cities and proclaimed himself King of the Hijaz and Sultan of Najd. In 1932, his new realm was re-named Saudi Arabia.

Throughout the 1920s, Transjordan made considerable progress in modernising its infrastructure. 1928 saw the writing of a constitution and the establishment of a legislative council. By 1939, a regular cabinet was in place. While Britain was still in control of financial and military matters, British colonial policies were being relaxed, and Transjordanian consular representatives were being stationed in Arab countries. The emirate was on a path toward full independence.

Meanwhile, Hitler had come to power in 1933. As if on cue, the British-appointed Mufti of Jerusalem, Hajj Amin al-Husseini, openly declared his support for the dictator. When the Peel Commission

offered a plan for the partition of Palestine into an Arab state, consisting of Transjordan and Arab Palestine and a Jewish homeland, the mufti, who officially represented the Palestinians, rejected the proposal Abdullah, however, voted in its favour. When Britain issued the 1939 White Paper along the lines of the 1937 Peel commission recommendations, the Emir of Transjordan was the only Arab leader who accepted the partition plan. This set the tone for the future relationships between Jordan, its Arab neighbours, the West and Israel.

During World War II, Transjordan entered the conflict on the side of Britain and aided in the overthrow of Iraq's pro-Axis government of Rashid Ali al-Gaylani in 1941. Both, Gaylani and the Mufti of Jerusalem subsequently fled to Berlin. Transjordanian Arab Legion troops were also deployed to guard British interests in Egypt. Towards the end of the war, a series of summit meetings of Arab heads of state culminated in the creation of the Arab League, an organisation designed to streamline Arab regional policy. One of the League's fundamental principles outlined at its inception by the founding members Transjordan, Egypt, Syria, Lebanon, Saudi Arabia, Iraq and Yemen was that no Arab country should take up arms against another.

In March 1946, the Treaty of London delineated nominal independence for the Emirate of Transjordan and on the 25th of the same month the country's name was officially changed to the Hashemite Kingdom of Jordan with Abdullah I as its sovereign. But the future of the new state was increasingly becoming entwined with the question of Palestine.

The struggle between Palestinians and Jews had reached crisis proportions in the wake of Jewish mass immigration during World War II and immediately after. Despite its considerable military presence, Britain found itself unable to control the region and handed the thorny problem over to the United Nations. On the 29th of November 1947, the UN General Assembly passed a resolution calling for the partition of Palestine into an Arab and a Jewish state, and the placement of the city of Jerusalem under international jurisdiction. The ruling was accepted by the Jewish leadership, but the Arab League unanimously rejected the partition. Fighting broke out immediately and escalated into full-scale war with the arrival of the Arab League's Army of Deliverance in January 1948.

The British relinquished their mandate over Palestine on the 15th of May, hours after the declaration of an independent state of Israel. Hostilities intensified and significant territorial gains were made by the Jordanian Arab Legion under the command of Glubb Pasha. When the war came to an end in the spring of 1949, Jordan was in possession of the West Bank and the eastern part of Jerusalem, constituting a large part of the Arab state envisaged by 1947 UN resolution. In 1950, elections were held in Jordan, inviting the Palestinian population to participate fully in the political process. The West Bank was constitutionally annexed to the Hashemite Kingdom, thus increasing its territory considerably, and its population by over a million people.

On 20th July 1951, during his regular Friday visit to the al-Aqsa mosque in East Jerusalem, Islam's "furthermost sanctuary" from which the Prophet, accompanied by the Angel Gabriel, was said

Modern bridge crossing the Wadi Mujib on the eastern shores of the Dead Sea.

to have made the Night Journey to the throne of God, King Abdullah I was assassinated by a young Palestinian. This tragic murder was witnessed by his teenage grandson Hussein. Subsequently, the crown passed to Abdullah's son Talal. In 1952 he abdicated in favour of his eldest son Hussein, then only seventeen years of age. Hussein formally acceded to the Hashemite throne on the 2nd of May 1953, to begin a 47 year long reign. This period in Jordanian history was to be almost entirely overshadowed by the Palestine-Israel conflict.

Jordan had been in possession of the West Bank since the close of the first Arab-Israeli war, investing substantially in its development. The fertile agricultural lands were becoming an integral part of the Jordanian economy, while the ubiquitous presence of historic sites significant to Jews, Christians and Muslims alike allowed for the tentative growth of a Holy Land tourist industry. Nonetheless, over 500,000 Palestinian refugees flooded across the Jordan River to live in refugee-camps administered by the United Nations Relief and Works Agency (UNWRA). Traumatised and despondent, these people had lost their land, their homes and their national identity through international intrigue and imperial fiat. The scene was set for diverse radical groups, under the mantle of pan-Arab unity, to vie for their membership. The annexation of the West Bank by Jordan had only been recognised internationally by the governments of Britain and Pakistan, whilst the general consensus, especially in the Arab world, condemned it.

Jordan was still closely tied to Britain by treaty, its state coffers subsidised by the British crown whilst the Jordanian army remained under the command of Glubb Pasha. In light of this status quo and the mounting criticism from the Arab world, general discontent began to grow in the military, and amongst the wider population. The young King Hussein inevitably bowed to both external and internal pressures demanding his disassociation from the British, and dismissed Glubb Pasha in early 1956 as head of his armed forces. In mid-July of the same year, Gamal Abdul Nasser, president of the newly established Republic of Egypt, nationalised the Suez Canal and precipitated an international crisis that culminated in the Israeli occupation of Sinai and the deployment of French and British troops to Port Said. The Suez Crisis accelerated Britain's and France's colonial decline, with Washington stepping in and demanding the unconditional withdrawal of the three aggressor nations' forces.

Since the close of World War II, the United States of America had emerged as the world's new dominant superpower. The Americans had been steadily increasing their influence in the Middle East, implementing an ill-disguised strategy to oust the colonialists by openly supporting pan-Arab nationalist movements. They sought military and strategic alliances offering economic aid to Middle Eastern countries threatened by communism (Eisenhower Doctrine 1957).

In the light of diminishing British financial support, King Hussein expressed his interest in American aid. However, a few months earlier, a pro-Nasserite government had been elected in Amman. It broke off diplomatic relations with France, abrogated the Anglo-Jordanian treaty and intended formally to recognise the Soviet Union and Communist China. On the 10th of April, the new government was forced to resign, resulting in demonstrations throughout the country and leading to an attempted coup. A state of emergency

Today modern carriages transport goods from Aqaba to Amman on the old Hijaz Railway Line built by German engineers in the first decade of the 20th century.

was declared, reinforced by the declaration of martial law. During this period, the last British troops finally withdrew from Jordan.

Jordan became increasingly isolated amongst Arab States and bore the brunt of an intense propaganda war being waged by Gamal Abdul Nasser of Egypt, who had emerged as the champion of the pan-Arab cause and principal supporter of the anti-British Ba'ath party of Syria. Relations with Syria and Egypt became progressively strained, especially after the two countries jointly formed the United Arab Republic in 1958. In response Jordan entered a similar union with Iraq, creating an Arab Federation. The latter was short lived. Six months after its inauguration, the federation was dissolved by a bloody coup which overthrew (and massacred) the ruling Hashemite family in Baghdad, proving disastrous to Jordanian economic and political interests. Iraqi oil supplies to Jordan were cut off and observers at the time believed that the Jordanian royal family would soon share the fate of their Iraqi cousins. But the 23-year-old Jordanian monarch emerged as a tenacious and intelligent statesman far beyond his years who would, time after time, prove both pundits and detractors wrong during the course of his long reign.

In 1960 King Hussein granted full citizenship to all Palestinians living within Jordan. Despite the precarious internal and regional political climate, the sixties gave rise to a new liberal professional class comprised to a large extent of Jordanians of Palestinian origin deeply committed to building a modern society. The potash, phosphate and cement industries developed during this decade; a new oil refinery was constructed; and the first national university was founded. As the population increased, water became a key polit-

ical issue. This was aggravated in 1963 by the Israeli government's announcement of its intention to divert water from the Jordan River to the Negev Desert. At the same time diverse radical opposition groups, united by common hatred of the Israeli occupation of Palestine, continued to converge on Jordan.

During a summit of Arab leaders in Cairo in January 1964, the Arab League countered Israel's intentions by proposing to rechannel some of the Lebanese and Syrian tributaries to Lake Tiberias. The same conference also saw the creation of a joint Arab military force, composed of Egyptian, Syrian and Lebanese troops as well as the establishment of the Palestine Liberation Organisation (PLO), nominally under Arab League control. The PLO's headquarters were to be in Amman. This was followed by the first Palestine National Congress in Jerusalem four month later, hosted by King Hussein. Aside from placing Jordan firmly on the side of Arab leaders, the conference also opened the door to an unchecked influx of *fedayeen* (Palestinan combatants) into the country. Within two years, Amman was unable to control *fedayeen* raids from Jordan into Israel.

Israel retaliated against the mounting threats and intimidation, and in June 1967 launched an all-out military offensive against its Arab neighbours. In a surprise pre-emptive strike heralding the start of the Six Day War, the Egyptian air force was destroyed on the ground, whilst Syrian ground forces were swiftly pushed back to the outskirts of Damascus. The Jordanian army, the best trained and most disciplined fighting force in the Arab world, was pressured into a major military counterattack against superior Israeli firepower. By the time a UN ceasefire brought a halt to six days of fighting, Israel

had occupied the Egyptian Sinai, Syria's Golan Heights, and the entire Jordanian West Bank, including Arab East Jerusalem and the Gaza Strip. As a result, a further 300,000 Palestinians lost their homes and fled to Jordan. Despite UN resolution 242 calling for the *"withdrawal of Israeli armed forces from territories occupied during the recent conflict"*, the occupation continues to this day.

Jordan was hard hit by the 1967 war. 70% of its agricultural land and a significant part of its industry had been located in the West Bank. The loss of Jerusalem and other holy sites had a devastating effect on its tourist industry. The massive influx of new Palestinian immigrants, coupled with the rising presence of militant *fedayeen* groups threw Jordan into a state of near-anarchy. The country was further destabilised and on the brink of civil war, as radical Arab leaders mounted vitriolic attacks against the Hashemite regime. Hijackings, assassination attempts, riots and open confrontations between the *fedayeen* and the army escalated into the "Black September" of 1970, coming to a head with in the ill-disguised Syrian invasion. A vigorous defence by King Hussein's military saw off the Syrians, and the PLO was expelled from Jordan, with its radical elements forcefully repressed by the army. The king had survived the greatest threat yet to his kingdom and his rule. The following two decades saw the strengthening of his authority both internally, as a competent head of state, and internationally, as a key player in regional politics.

When Egypt and Syria launched a surprise military offensive against Israel on October 6th 1973 – the Yom Kippur or Ramadan war – Jordan remained officially neutral. In spite of initial successes, the devastating defeat of the two Arab countries by Israel produced regional political turmoil, leading to the suspension of oil exports by Arab oil producing countries to the US, its Western European allies and Japan, causing the "oil shock" of 1973. By the following year, the price of oil on the world market had quadrupled, initiating a period of economic recession in the noncommunist industrial world and a significant shift by Western Europe and Japan to more pro-Arab policies.

In 1974 Jordan recognised the PLO as the *"'sole legitimate representative of the Palestinian people"*. King Hussein dissolved parliament and elections, suspending the participation of Palestinians from the West Bank in the Jordanian political process until the resolution of the West Bank question. Nonetheless, the 1970s saw some stability return to Jordan. Domestic policy aimed to promote national unity, while integrating Palestinian refugees into a modern Jordanian society in its struggle to rebuild the economy. Remittances sent back by Palestinian Jordanians working in the Gulf States brought considerable revenue during the oil-boom years. The relocation of part of the regional Beirut financial sector, following the outbreak of the Lebanese civil war in 1975, provided a further boost to the Jordanian economy.

Negotiations between Egypt and Israel, spearheaded by the Americans, culminated in the Camp David Accords of 1978 and the return of Israeli-occupied Sinai to Egypt. As a result, Egypt was expelled from the Arab League. Jordan, like most other Arab countries, broke all relations with Egypt, with Jordanian elections being postponed indefinitely.

Today truck drivers not camel caravans stop for rest and refuelling at Azraq before venturing through the desert to Iraq, or conversely to Amman or Aqaba.

During the eight-year Iran-Iraq war, Jordan supported Iraq, its principal supplier of discounted oil. The old Mesopotamian overland trade route of Aqaba-Azraq-Baghdad became the primary supply line to the Iraqi military, enriching the Jordanian economy. While tensions mounted once again with Syria (which backed Iran during this period, in return for cheap Iranian oil), relations were prudently restored with Egypt.

In the light of growing internal discontent, parliament was reconvened in 1984 and full political rights were restored to the "Palestinian-Jordanians" of the West Bank. This in turn evoked fierce protest from the Palestine Liberation Organisation, which interpreted the move as an attack on its position as the "sole representative of the Palestinian people". A resolution of the Israel-Palestine question thus became ever more critical to lasting peace in the region.

In 1985, King Hussein skilfully negotiated the Amman Accord with the PLO, amounting to a commitment to enter peace negotiations with Israel. The following year, however, the acknowledged leader of the organisation, Yasser Arafat, bowed to pressure from opposing Palestinian groups and reneged on the agreement. In October 1987, a popular uprising – the first *Intifada*, sometimes also called the "war of stones" – broke out in the Israeli occupied territories on the West Bank and the Gaza Strip, postponing peace through negotiation. It also gave ammunition to right-wing elements in Israel, who had been actively lobbying for transformation of the East Bank (Jordanian territory) into an alternative homeland for all Palestinians. In reaction to this political impasse, King Hussein dissolved parliament again in 1988 and formally renounced all claims

to the West Bank. A year later, the first elections since 1967 were held (Jordanian women voting for the first time), followed by the lifting of martial law.

The 1990 invasion of Kuwait by Iraq and the first Gulf War presented a considerable strategic dilemma for Jordan. Commerce and free oil supplied by Iraq were vital to the weak Jordanian economy, whilst a majority of the Palestinian population sympathised with Saddam Hussein's radical anti-Israeli regime. Nonetheless, in compliance with UN sanctions, all trade with Iraq came to a halt, though prevailing Jordanian public sentiment prevented the Hashemite Kingdom in joining the anti-Iraq coalition. At the same time, the influx of over a million refugees, of which 300,000 settled permanently in Jordan, increased the strains on finances, water supply and social infrastructure to bursting point.

The 1991 Madrid conference initiated a series of negotiations over the Israel-Palestine question, leading to the signing of 1993 Oslo Accords, a declaration of principles on interim self-government arrangements delineating Israel's conditional withdrawal from the Gaza Strip and the West Bank, to be administered by the newly established Palestinian National Authority (PNA).

A year later, the Washington Declaration officially terminated the state of war between Israel and Jordan, preparing the way for the normalisation of relations between the two sovereign nation states. The treaty was formally signed and celebrated on the Wadi Araba border crossing between Jordan and Israel on 26th October 1994, outlining a number of land, water and border agreements. But the assassination of the Israeli Prime Minister Yizhak Rabin in

November 1995 precipitated a swing to the extreme right in Israeli politics, bringing with it a pervasive sense of disillusionment amongst the Palestinians.

On the 28th of September 2000 the second *Intifada* began. The catalyst was provided by the brutal attack on Palestinian protesters by Israeli troops on the steps of the al-Aqsa Mosque. Tragically, the uprising continues to date and is marked by exceptional violence and loss of life on both sides.

On the 7th February 1999 King Hussein of Jordan finally succumbed in his battle with cancer. His rule had spanned 47 years of tempestuous Middle Eastern politics, and his death was genuinely and deeply mourned, both at home and abroad. An astute politician, King Hussein had successfully administered a kingdom with little resources, surviving numerous attempts on his life, invasions by Israel and Syria, internal strife and constant external pressures. When he died at the age of 64, he bequeathed a legacy of decency and common sense, to which few 20th century Middle Eastern potentates could lay claim. Jordan today owes an immeasurable debt to the 17-year old boy who truly would be king. He was succeeded by his 37-year-old son, Abdullah, former commander of Jordan's Special Forces.

When his grandfather, Abdullah I, arrived in Ma'an in 1920, Jordan's population had numbered no more than 400,000. Less than a century later, Abdullah II inherited a country of over 5 million inhabitants of diverse origins, predominantly urban and well educated, striving to define its identity and destiny in the 21st century.

Economic reforms, instigated during the last years of King Hussein's rule, have been continued by his son. Jordan's membership of the World Trade Organisation since 2000, the signing of a US-Jordan Free Trade agreement in 2001 and the EU-Jordan trade association agreement the following year have been seen as significant steps towards sustaining growth. The government is gradually liberalising and deregulating the economy, increasingly attracting foreign investment primarily in the property and construction markets, while tourism and the mineral industry bring further valuable revenue. The Dead Sea area, with its natural hot springs, ancient sites and luxury leisure developments, has been targeted by the so-called "curative tourist industry". Similarly, Aqaba's special economic zone has been selected for ambitious future projects along Jordan's southern coast, the port area and the town proper.

Jordan's most valuable asset, however, is its highly qualified, young (and relatively inexpensive) workforce. The service sector accounts for two thirds of the total GNP output, with banking, education, health and pharmaceuticals closely tied to the service

King Hussein proudly confers honours to his son Abdullah (left), *the future king of the Hashemite Kingdom of Jordan.*

Celebrations commending Jordanian high-school students of excellence in the restored South Theatre at Jarash (right) *on the eve of Independence Day, the 25th May 2004.*

industry. Information technology (IT) has been given special attention, and an IT-based private sector is expanding rapidly.

The US-led war on Iraq in 2003 dealt another major economic blow to Jordan, which was dependent on discounted oil from its Iraqi neighbour. While several Gulf nations have in the meantime provided temporary aid, Jordan faces a difficult future in terms of its lack of two vital resources: oil and water. Economic growth is thus fundamental to its survival, a growth that is ultimately determined by regional and internal stability.

In order to promote the kind of national solidarity essential to the kingdom's future success, a campaign with the motto "Jordan First" was initiated by King Abdullah II in October 2002. Its concept and the proposed implementation mechanisms are nothing if not ambitious. Quintessentially a formula for a new philosophy of governance, the Jordan First campaign emphasises the pre-eminence of Jordan's national interests, and aims to reformulate the state-individual relationship. It proposes a gradual liberalisation process towards a fully democratic society, rallying support for this process from all strata of the population. In an open letter to the Jordanian prime minister, Ali Abdul Ragheb, on the 30th of October 2002, King

Abdullah underlined his belief that "*'Jordan First' must be the common denominator between all Jordanians regardless of their origins, orientations, views, talents, faiths or races. This concept must be rendered into tangible reality and an act of free will. It should be established by the family, to begin with, school, university, youth centres, and private and public institutions*". Since this announcement, a 31 member strong national body to supervise the implementation of the political brief has been named while economic, social and political reform programmes are being developed to translate this concept into reality.

The Hashemite Kingdom of Jordan is a young country with a long history shaped by its unique geographic position as a nexus between diverse civilisations. Its strength throughout recorded history has been its ability to incorporate and synthesise – an ability now needed more than ever to ensure its economic wellbeing, social health and national survival for the centuries to come.

Light

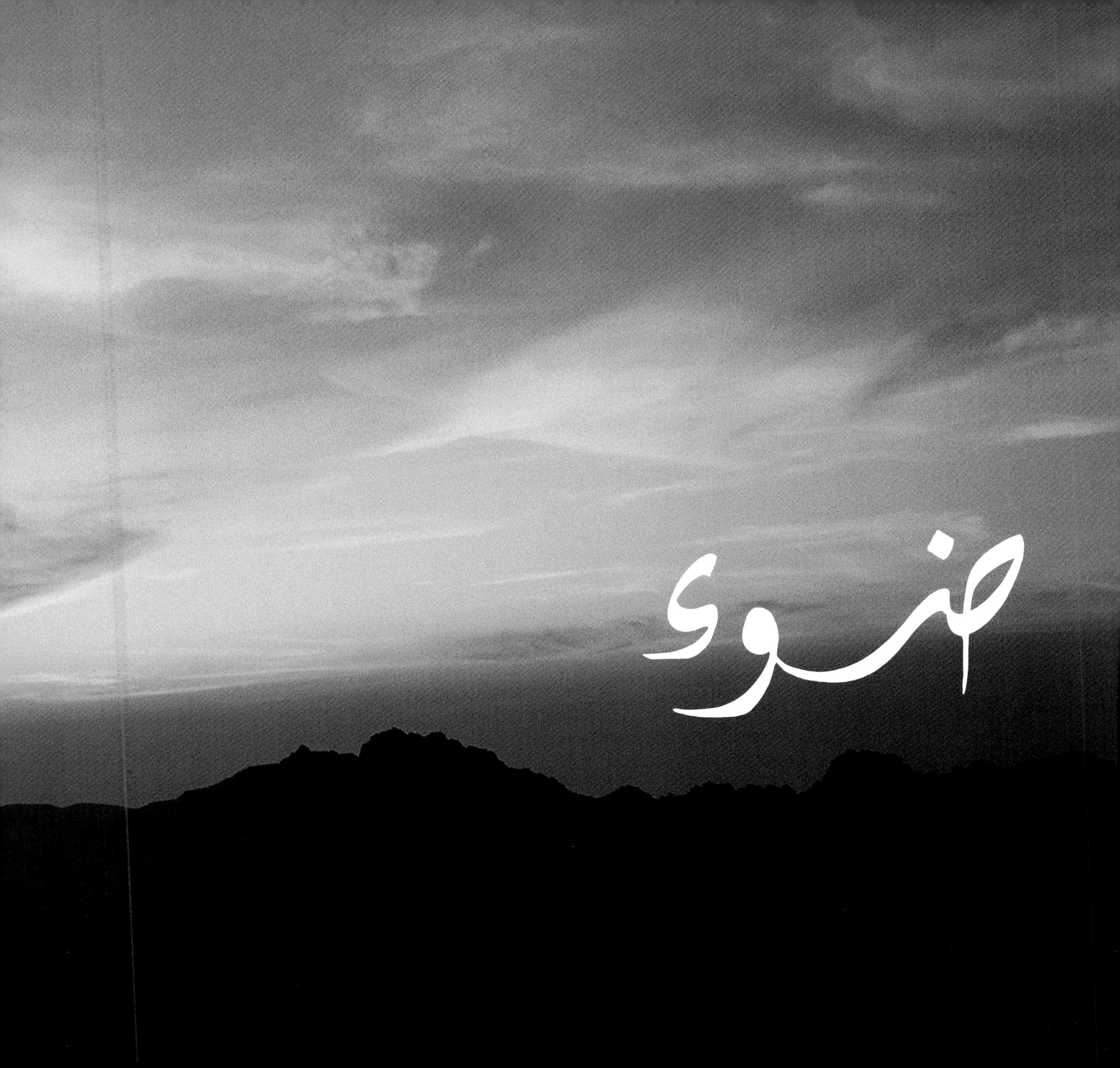
ضوء

(previous page) *An expansive panorama of mountains near Petra.*

(right) *The setting sun silhouettes two skeletal trees in the Dana Nature Reserve. Established by Jordan's environmental agency, the Royal Society for the Conservation of Nature (RSCN), this 320 square mile reserve near the King's Highway south of Tafila is home to some 600 plant species and 200 species of birds.*

Desert Thistles add golden hues to the arid Jordanian summer landscape.

Jordan – A Timeless Land

Flint and limestone outcrops contrasting with the Thulaithawat Mountains; the reflecting surface of the hard flint gives the desert an ephemeral sheen.

Columns of the
Civic Complex
(left), *once the
centre of ancient
Pella. Pella is
amongst the
earliest inhabited
sites in Jordan,
and was
mentioned in
Egyptian
documents in the
14th century* BC
*as a source of
contractors for
chariot wheels.*

*The Treasury
(right)* provides
a spectacular
greeting for
visitors as they
emerge from the
narrow confines
of the Siq into
the "rose-red city"
of Petra.

(left) *Ranks of steps at the restored Roman Theatre in Amman were carved out of the hillside in the waning days of the Nabataean trading empire to accommodate 6,000 spectators.*

(right) *Sunset over the Dead Sea.*

Lone horseman leading his steed through the breathtaking landscape of Wadi Musa.

(above) *Over thousands of years, the soft sandstone of the Jabal Umm Fruth has eroded to form a natural bridge in the far south of Wadi Rum.*

(left) *Wadi Rum is punctuated by mountains rising from the desert with Jabal Rum reaching a height of 1,754m. In 1998, the Royal Society for the Conservation of Nature (RSCN) established the Wadi Rum Protected Area.*

Sunset silhouettes the mountains surrounding Wadi Musa (Valley of Moses) (left), a thriving modern town on the approaches to Petra. Here, Moses is said to have struck a rock with his rod and water flowed from it – as it still does today from Moses Spring.

Siq al Barid (left), also known as the Wadi Dhalma, a lesser known entrance to the natural fortress of Pella.

Air & Water

(previous page) *An infinity pool at one of the hotels on the eastern bank of the Dead Sea appears to blend into the mineral-rich waters of the lowest place on earth. The landlocked sea extends 65 kilometres along the border between Jordan and Israel.*

An A310-300 Airbus (right), one of the fleet belonging to the national carrier, Royal Jordanian Airline, overflies the mountains of southern Jordan, touching down in Aqaba en route from Amman to London.

The majestic profile of the Golden Eagle (below).

Masters of the sky: the Steppe Eagle (above), *the most common migratory eagle in Jordan and the Saker Falcon* (left) *with it's prey of ferral pigeon.*

Spotted Box Fish

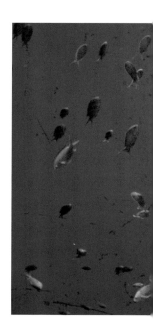

Parrot Fish

Lion Fish

The Spanish Dancer

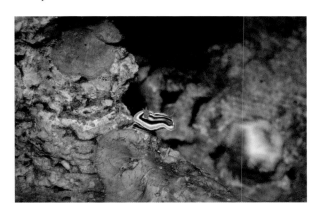

A blaze of colour greets scuba divers in the Red Sea, home to over 400 species of coral and 1,000 species of fish, some of which are unique to these waters, such as the Parrot fish (above left) *which envelopes it's in a membrane to fool potential predators.*

Lyretail Coralfish (left)

Goldfinch

The Azraq wetlands (left) are a
popular winter residence for migratory
water fowl, including the graceful
Grey Heron (below)

Sinai Rose Finch

The European Bee-Eater (right), *is an annual visitor to the Jordan Rift Valley.*

Barn Owl (left)

Common Kingfisher (right)

Cattle Egret (below)

Detail of Iris Bismarckiana (left), *a newly discovered specie of wild Iris, found only in a small area of the Dibeen National Park, north-west of Amman. Jordan has one of the highest diversities of wild flowers in the world. The Spiny Broom (right)* is common to the hills of the Jordan Rift Valley; the *Purple Clover (second right)* is found in most mediterranean mountains; the *Black Iris (far right), the national flower of Jordan, becomes the object of pilgrimage for two weeks every spring.*

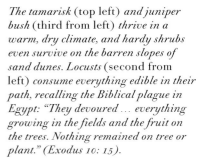

The tamarisk (top left) and juniper bush (third from left) thrive in a warm, dry climate, and hardy shrubs even survive on the barren slopes of sand dunes. Locusts (second from left) consume everything edible in their path, recalling the Biblical plague in Egypt: "They devoured … everything growing in the fields and the fruit on the trees. Nothing remained on tree or plant." (Exodus 10: 15).

It is commonly believed that Christ's thorny crown was wrought from the spikey Ziziphus jujuba tree (above right).

White Saxaul (left) surviving in the dunes of Wadi Rum. A small stand of eucalyptus trees (right) towers over the visitors' centre at Petra.

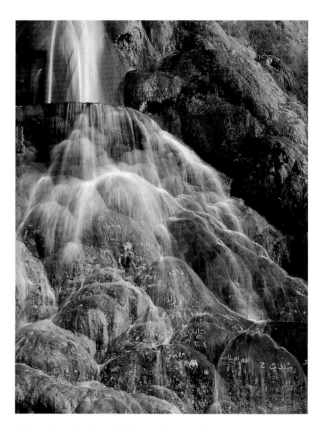

Throughout Jordan, hidden springs and waterfalls provide respite from the desert heat: Hammamat Ma'in is a popular bathing spot (above and top left) *fed by about 60 thermal springs; the cool waters of Wadi Mujib* (left and right) *rush through a steep gorge towards the Dead Sea.*

(previous page) *Bathers wallow in the Dead Sea 410m (1,300ft) below sea level. Evaporation creates a high concentration of salt and minerals, famous for their healing and restorative properties.*

Horseman resting by the river.

Sometimes called the Grand Canyon of Jordan, the four kilometre-wide valley of Wadi Mujib transforms abruptly into a narrow gorge.

Dead Sea salt formations create
unearthly landscapes.

Land

(previous page) *Named after the book by T. E. Lawrence, the Seven Pillars of Wisdom stand like unyielding sentinels near the entrance to Wadi Rum.* (right) *Awed by the majesty of the landscape, Lawrence wrote: "In truth I liked Rum too much. Rum the magnificent…vast, echoing and godlike."*

Megalithic chamber tombs (left) *uncovered by the passage of time. Dolmens, dating from the Early Bronze Age, can be found on both side of the Jordan Rift Valley.*

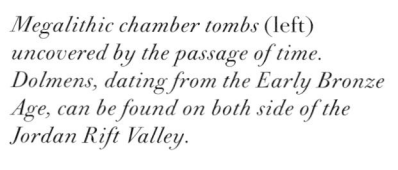

Via Nova Traiana (above), the northern section of the King's Highway approaching the old Nabataean trading capital of Bostra, situated just north of the present day border between modern Jordan and Syria.

King Herod the Great is said to have built his castle on the hilltop of Machaerus (left) near the village of Mukawir. It was here that his son and successor, Herod Antipas, agreed to Salome's request to have John the Baptist beheaded.

Ancient olive tree (above), such trees can date as far back as to Roman rule of the region 2000 years ago.

Snow covered fields (left) near Ajlun.

Arabian palm trees (right) growing wild in natural water channels.

(previous page)
Boulders in the Eastern Desert; these
concretions were formed around the
time of the extinction of the dinosaurs,
some 65 million years ago.

Rock layers in Mudawara (above)
in the southern deserts of Jordan are
an invaluable storehouse of scientific
information.

Sandstone formations (left) *in the mountains to the east of the Dead Sea. These differential erosions give the landscape a rich and beguiling texture.*

The Dead Sea (right) *is sinking into the slowly widening Rift Valley at a rate of about one metre annually.*

(far right) *Another bizarre sandstone composition*

Throughout Jordan numerous wildlife sanctuaries have been established by Jordan's Royal Society for the Conservation of Nature. The rare Nubian Ibex (top) can be found in the Mujib Reserve; the Asiatic or Golden Jackal (above) roams the Azraq Reserve once more; the Arabian Oryx (left) has been successfully bred in captivity in the Shaumari Reserve near Azraq. It is proudly displayed as the symbol of Jordan's RSCN.

The Stone Marten (right), *another endangered species, can still be found in the woodlands around Ajloun and Dibeen. The Water Buffalo* (below) *was introduced to Azraq by migrating Chechens, who settled in Jordan in 1902. Buffalo still help to clear the waterways by grazing in the reeds.*

Jordan – A Timeless Land

Wadi Dahek (left) in the eastern desert near the border between Jordan and Saudi Arabia.

Sandstone formations in the mountains to the east of the Dead Sea. These differential erosions give the landscape a rich and beguiling texture.

The Hawk's Beard, a hardy desert plant.

Locals harvest olives (left and right) near Jarash in September. The olive tree (Olea europaea) is the most important tree crop grown in Jordan, providing a source of income for thousands of families and seasonal jobs for agricultural workers. There are about 15 million olive trees in Jordan, producing nearly 200,000 tons of fruit, 86 percent of which is turned into olive oil.

Bedouin woman (above) *foraging for her livestock in the Jordan Valley.*

A watering point for sheep and goats (right). *Jordan is one of the world's most water-scarce countries. Two thirds of the country is desert or semi-desert. Besides subterranean aquifers, the Jordan and Yarmuk Rivers provide the only sources of this precious commodity.*

A Bedouin looks across the mountains towards Jaba' Haroun (Mount Hor) (top) where Prophet Aaron, the older brother of Moses, is said to have died at the age of 123 years, and is presumed buried. (Numbers 33: 39-40). Family picnic (right) in Alisheh Forest, overlooking the Yarmuk River.

Colour

Striated sandstone (left) forms the ceiling of a Nabataean tomb chamber in Petra. Flowering Woody Spurge (above) emblazon the hills around Ajlun. Ajlun Castle (right) resplendent in spring with the Catchfly Flower.

Pink Rock Rose (top)
Storax Tree Flower (above)
Mistletoe (above left)
The very rare Sodada Caper (left)
The common Poppy (far left)

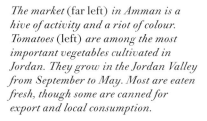

The market (far left) in Amman is a hive of activity and a riot of colour. Tomatoes (left) are among the most important vegetables cultivated in Jordan. They grow in the Jordan Valley from September to May. Most are eaten fresh, though some are canned for export and local consumption.

A pile of rugs (right) fades against the sunlight outside a shop in Petra.

Colourfully painted trucks (below) are a traditional carry-over into contemporary times, derived from the rich decorated livery and saddle bags of camels.

(above) *Sold on the street in Amman, the delicious bread-like* Kaek *is a popular snack.*

(above right) *Sacks of herbs and spices on sale outside a shop in downtown Amman.*

Camels have been held in high regard since the age of caravan trade and are still adorned with rich colourful fabrics, redolent of this ancient tradition. (below) Bedouin seat cushion covers decorated with traditional Arabic designs.

(above) *Azraq Castle (Qasr al-Azraq) was constructed of local basalt around* AD 300. *The Arabic inscription over the main entrance indicates substantial rebuilding in* AD 1237. *It was here that T. E. Lawrence and Prince Feisal were based in the winter of 1917 during the Arab Revolt against the Ottoman Empire. Each spring, the castle is surrounded by a carpet of colourful wildflowers.*

(left) *Ubiquitous in Jordan, the Hibiscus explodes in a riot of colours.*

Six-spot Burnet (above)
Palestine Marbled White (top right)
Cetonia (Scarabaeidae) (left)

Weaver drying his freshly dyed wool outside his shop in Madaba (above), *contrasts with the real supplier* (right). *The Toothed Orchid* (far right) *is a rare and endangered species restricted to the northern forests of Jordan.*

Blue Sinai Agama (above)
Yellow Asphodel (left)

The Temple of Hercules (left) *on Citadel Hill, Amman. Hammamat Ma'in* (above) *near Madaba*

Ancients

قديم

(previous page) *The Street of Façades along the Outer Siq in Petra presents a group of 44 carved façades on four levels that were probably used as dwellings by the Nabataeans.*

(above and right) *The frescoes in the audience hall of the Umayyad-built Qusayr Amra in eastern Jordan depict a variety of scenes, including a nude woman bathing, amorini, garden and hunting scenes, animals and craftsmen. Qusayr Amra is famous for its bath complex, and is included in UNESCO's World Heritage List.*

The Bedouin (right) *were originally desert dwellers and make up a large proportion of Jordan's indigenous population.*

The Corinthian Tomb (left), *carved into the East Cliff Jabal al-Khubtha in Petra, includes three small chambers and one large room.*

Carved caves and archways opposite the Theatre in Petra (right).

Traditional 19th century manor house (above) *on the outskirts of Amman.*

Reconstructed pillars of Machaerus (left), *Herod the Great's castle near Mukawir.*

Ancient olive tree (right) *in the vicinity of the village of Tibna in northern Jordan. Knarled old trees like this one are often revered as* wali, *believed to be the seat of the spirit of a holy man and imbued with supernatural power.*

*The restored 2nd-century Roman
Theatre in Amman* (right) *is still used
for performances today. Nobles used
to sit in the first of the three sections,
followed by the military and by
ordinary citizens, seated at the top.*

*Nabataean inscriptions on the
Turkmaniyya tomb (above) in the
Umm Saihoun area of Petra. This long
inscription gives an inventory of tomb
features, such as the cambers, loculi,
courtyard, etc. and a dedication to the
Nabataean god Dushara.*

Carved blocks of stone await restoration work (above) at Qasr al-Bint in Petra, one of many restoration projects breathing new life into Jordan's historical sites and treasures.

Inscription on a stone slab (right) in the Archaeological Park in Madaba.

Architectural decorative details (below) from the Nabataean and Roman periods.

The Pharaoh's Treasury in Petra as rendered by David Roberts in 1859.

The Monastery (Al-Deir) (right) in Petra is larger than the Treasury and is topped with a large free-standing urn flanked by two half pediments.

This Byzantine tower near Umm al Rasas (left) *may have served as a lofty hermitage for a stylite monk.*

Umm al-Jimal (above), *black basalt city on the edge of the Hauran.*

Jarash Cardo (right) *near the Artemis Gate.*

View through the doorway of a traditional house onto fields of wheat and olive groves on the outskirts of Ma'in village (above).

The main entrance to the Hellenistic palace of Qasr al-Abd (left), *the Palace of the Servant, west of Amman.*

Part of the Urn Tomb (above), one of the Royal Tombs in Petra named after the urn finial carved over the upper pediment. Probably built in about AD 70, the large main chamber was used as a Byzantine church in the 5th century, and bears a Greek dedication with the date AD 446-47.

The theatre in Petra (right) was carved from solid rock by the Nabataeans in the 1st century AD. The 45 rows originally seated about 3,000 spectators. This was enlarged by the Romans to accommodate about 8,500 in AD 106, after their annexation of Nabataea to the Province of Arabia.

One of several caves in the hillside of Mukawir (above), where John the Baptist was said to have been imprisoned and executed by Herod Antipas, successor to Herod the Great.

Qasr Tuba (left), an unfinished Umayyad desert palace located in a remote valley in the Eastern Desert.

Detail of the rare brickwork (below), typical of Persian building techniques

Hamman as-Sarah (right), an early Islamic bath complex near Qasr Hallabat, one of the largest Umayyad desert castles.

Umm-Masrab Byzantine church (above) *near the Jordanian-Syrian border. Shobak Crusader Castle* (left, right).

Roman Temple (left) *in Dhat Ras*

Early 16th-century Arabic relief inscriptions (right) *on the wall inside the entrance gate of the partially reconstructed Aqaba Fort. On the right it reads "blessed and auspicious fort our Lord the ruling Sultan al-Malik al-Ashraf abu al-Nassar Qansawh al Gharwi, Sultan of Islam and the Muslims, slayer of the unbelievers and the polytheists" and continues on the left "receiver of justice in the universe... the sultan... may God glorify his victories through Muhammad and his house! This blessed fort was the work of the Amir Khayir Bey al-'Ala the builder."*

Detail of Qatrana (above), *Ottoman Hajj fort along the Desert Highway to Mecca.*

Old man grazing his goats (left) *amongst the remains of a Nabataean temple complex at the village of Dhat Ras, north of Karak.*

Ruins of the marketplace (macellum) in Jarash include a pillar with a Greek inscription (from the "traders"), erected during in the 2nd century AD. The macellum is flanked by two fountains; the northern one is inscribed with a dedication to Julia Domna, one of the great women of the East.

In Petra, the Colonnaded Street passes through the three arches of the 2nd-century temenos or Monumental Gateway, marking the entrance to the sacred enclosure of the Qasr al-Bint temple (above).

The Greek Orthodox Church of St George in Madaba was built in 1896 over the remains of a Byzantine church. It is best known for the mosaic map on its floor, depicting major biblical sites between Lebanon and Egypt marked in Greek. Created around AD 560, only a third of the original two million-piece map survives.

Figurative mosaics (above, right and
top right) *in Petra's Byzantine Church,
excavated in 1992-3. The church was
originally built by the Nabataeans,
later modified and enlarged by during
the Byzantine periods.*

*The well-preserved mosaics in the
Moses Memorial Church, Mt. Nebo*
(top left and above) *features wine-
making and hunting scenes, with
a number of birds and animals.*

Built between AD 150 and 170, the temple of Artemis (above) in the well-preserved Roman provincial city of Jarash (Gerasa) is dedicated to the goddess of hunting and fertility.

The North Theatre (left) in Jarash was built in AD 165 for government meetings.

Columns of the 6th-century octagonal church in Gadara (right).

Inhabited for over 2,500 years, Wadi Rum lies on an ancient camel trading route to and from the Arabian Peninsula. Rock inscriptions (left) *mark the position of one of the caravan stations.*

The 8th-century Umayyad palace (above) *with its reconstructed dome at the Citadel on Jabal al-Qal'a in Amman and* (above right) *the palace viewed through the doorway of the governor's house.*

The elusive site of Sela has served as a refuge from the Bronze Age to the Mamlukes. Fantastic architectural remains can today be visited on the hidden high plateau (top and right), whilst ancient field systems are still used by the villagers of old Sela (above). Striations and swirls of colour naturally decorate the hewn rock caves of Petra (far right).

Faith

(previous page) *Near Mukawir south west of Madaba, the castle of Herod the Great, Machaerus, is known locally as Qala'at al-Meshneq or Gallows Castle. The reconstructed pillars on the summit of the 700 metre hill can be seen for miles around.*

The King Abdullah Mosque in Amman (left) *was completed in 1989 by the late King Hussein in memory of his grandfather King Abdullah bin al-Hussein, founder of the Hashemite Kingdom of Jordan. The vast, pillar-less, octagonal prayer hall can accommodate up to 7,000 worshippers. The chandelier suspended from the centre of the dome comprises three circles supporting 168 lights and ornamented with the koranic verse: "Allah is the light of the Heavens and the Earth".*

The distinctive blue dome of the King Abdullah Mosque (above) *is 31metres high and 35metres in diameter.*

Worshippers (right) *extend out across the street in front of the King Hussein Mosque in the old sector of Amman during Friday prayers.*

On the summit of Mount Nebo (left) overlooking the Dead Sea stands a modern bronze cross bearing a replica of the brazen serpent that God instructed Moses to erect on a pole to stop the plague, sent during the Exodus journey (Numbers 21: 8-9). This event, which is often connected with the copper mines of Wadi Feinan, is referred to in the New Testament: "Just as Moses lifted up the snake in the desert, so the Son of Man must be lifted up, that everyone who believes in him may have eternal life." (John 3: 14-15).

Stained glass windows (above) in the Moses Memorial Church.

Moses Memorial Church (right) on Mt Nebo marks the spot where Moses is said to have died. "The Lord told Moses 'Go up into the Abarim Range to Mount Nebo in Moab, across from Jericho, and view Canaan, the land I am giving to the Israelites as their own possession. There on the mountain that you have climbed you will die.'" (Deuteronomy 32: 48-50).

Minarets of the King Hussein Mosque, Amman (above), *built by King Abdullah I in 1924 on the original site of one of the earliest mosques in the world built in AD 634-644. Dome* (right) *in the inner courtyard of the King Hussein Mosque, Amman. Mosaic floor* (left) *in the Byzantine basilica of SS Cosmas and Damian, built in AD 533 in Jarash (Gerasa).*

In the Church of the Apostles in Madaba (above left) *a craftsman called Salaman created this mosaic in AD 568. The central figure is Thalassa (Greek for the sea), surrounded by fish, animals, birds, flowers and fruits.*

Greek Orthodox Church near the King Abdullah Mosque in Amman (above). *The majority of Jordan's registered Christians belong to the Greek Orthodox Church.*

*Built in 1961 by the immigrant
Circassian community of Amman
(above), the Abu Darwish Mosque
presents a striking contrast of white
and black stone and commands a
conspicuous position on the crest of
Jabal Ashrafiyeh, south of Downtown.*

*A small mosque near the thermal
springs at Hammamat Ma'in south-
west of Madaba (above right).*

Pride

Byzantine tombs (above) *at the Cave of the Seven Sleepers 10 kilometres east of Amman.*

The role of this desert patrol sergeant with his camel in Wadi Rum (right) *has evolved from the policing of dissident tribesmen to rescuing stray tourists. Today, armoured patrol vehicles have largely replaced camels except on ceremonial occasions, but the desert patrol still operate out of a beau geste-style fort built in the 1930s.*

The Artemis Gate in Jarash (above) *leads to the temple of Artemis via a magnificent stairway.*

Schoolchildren (right) *visit the Cave of the Seven Sleepers, or Ahl al-Kahf, located outside the village of Al-Raqim.*

A row of pillars flank the ruins of the Octagonal Church in Gadara/ Umm Qais.

Roman theatre in downtown Amman.

*Elaborate jewellery worn by
Jordanian-Palestinian woman in
traditional costume. The art of
jewellery making in the regions harks
back to the Stone Age.*

*Contrast the modern designs inspired
from local plants* (below).

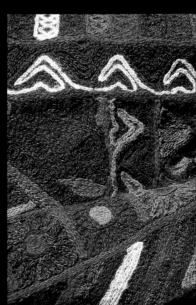

The tradition of Jordanian and Palestinian embroidery gave distinct identities to each villager.

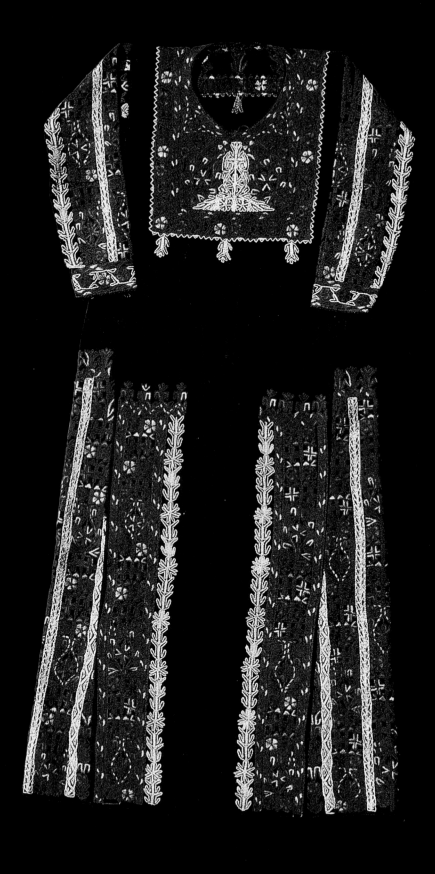

A Bedouin lady (above) clad in a protective head-scarf and goat's hair outer garment. Costume (right), of Bethlehem origin.

Local Bedouin leaders meet in the Dana Nature Reserve, one of many established by the Jordanian Royal Society for the Conservation of Nature (RSCN).

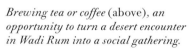

Brewing tea or coffee (above), *an opportunity to turn a desert encounter in Wadi Rum into a social gathering.*

A Bedouin (above right) *in the 15th-century stone village of Dana, currently being restored and re-inhabited through the efforts of the RSCN.*

A row of traditional coffee pots on display in Petra (far right).

Jordan – A Timeless Land

Bedouin guards (above) *stand by the imposing columns outside the entrance to the Treasury in Petra.*

Roman columns (left) *outside the Theatre form a backdrop to the bustle of life in Amman.*

King Abdullah II (above) *with his daughter Princess Salma.*

A Circassian dancer (left) *proudly displays his national costume. In 1878, the Circassians escaped persecution in the Russian Caucasus by migrating to Transjordan, and now over 30,000 of these non-Arab Muslims live in and around Amman in thriving communities.*

Moderns

Queen Rania (above), *champion of Jordan's youth, actively supports a number of social development programs. Jordan's population is just over 5 million, with nearly 50 percent under 16 years of age.*

The headquarters building (above) of the national carrier, Royal Jordanian Airline, in Amman.

Le Royal Hotel (left): contemporary Amman architecture using traditional building materials such as the ubiquitous limestone.

The Farah Hospital (right), *a modern construction incorporating Amman stone and glass.*

Typical 1960's neighbourhood in the capital city (below).

A family from Amman (above) *relaxes by the hotel pool beside the Dead Sea.*

The Queen of Jordan (top right) *at rest with two of her children in Aqaba.*

Set in one of the luxury hotels along the east coast of the Dead Sea, an infinity pool reflects the setting sun (left).

*Doctor's clinic in Irbid, flanked by
scribes who scratch a living from
writing letters dealing with officialdom
for the rural population.*

*Reflecting ancient 'Amman' stonework,
this building houses the Royal Society
for the Conservation of Nature
Museum.*

The Jordanian flag over Amman,
fluttering on the world's tallest flagpole.

Past and present merge effortlessly in the luxurious setting of the Aqaba's Mövenpick Hotel (above).

Boys playing with history in the ruins of the Nabataean temple of Dhat Ras (left).

The 3rd Circle, or King Talal Square, illustrates modern Amman's thriving cosmopolitan nature (right).

Joy

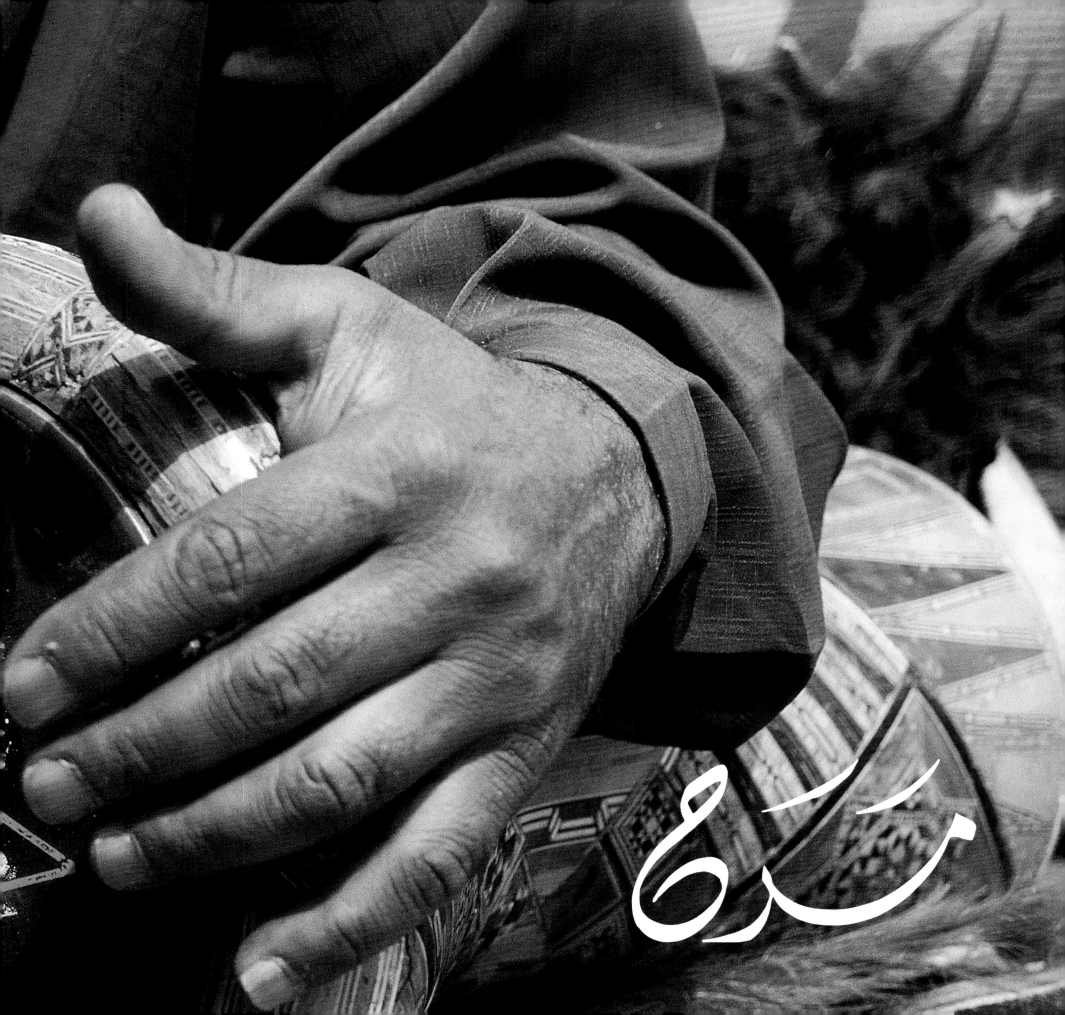

مَدّْح

(previous page) *Tabla, the traditional Arab drum.*

Wadi Rum is home to about 5,000 Bedouin, mostly of the Huweitat tribe. Many live in traditional goats' hair tents called bayt ash-sha'ar *– literally "house of hair". They raise camels, sheep and goats, but, today, much of their livelihood comes from tourism.*

The word Bedu means "nomadic".
This Bedouin family near Little Petra
(Siq Barid) live a semi-nomadic,
pastoral lifestyle tending to sheep, goats
and a donkey.

Music, poetry and story telling were encouraged in the courts of the Caliphs as a form of entertainment, especially by the Umayyads.

Jordan – A Timeless Land

Young horsemen in Petra prepare to hire out their services carrying tourists around the Nabataean city (left).

A camelier returns home along Petra's paved Colonnaded Street that follows the standard Roman pattern of an east-west decumanus, *which was once lined with shops* (right).

(following page) *The lines of the roof of this black, goat-hair Bedouin tent resemble the outlines of sandstone mountains in Wadi Rum.*

Credits

Index

Index

Selected Bibliography and Further Reading

Auge, C. and Dentzer, J.-M. *Petra: The Rose-Red City*, London, 2000

Bailey, C. *Jordan's Palestinian Challenge, 1948-1983: A Political History*, Colorado, 1984

Ball, W. *Rome in the East: The Transformation of an Empire*, London and New York, 2000.

Bell, G. *The Desert and the Sown*, London, 1907

Bienkowski, P. *The Art of Jordan*, Alan Sutton, 1991

Bienkowski, P. (ed.) *Early Edom and Moab*, Sheffield, 1992

Bowersock, G. W. *Roman Arabia*, Harvard University Press, 1983

Browning, I. *Jerash and the Decapolis*, Chatto and Windus, 1982

Browning I. *Petra*, Chatto and Windus, 1986

Burckhardt, J.L. *Travels in Syria and the Holy Land*, London 1882

Crone, P. *Meccan Trade and the Rise of Islam*, Princeton, 1987

Donnan, G. *The Kings Highway*, Jordan, 1994

Doughty, C.M. *Travels in Arabia Deserta*, London, 1888

Ferguson, J. *The Religions of the Roman Empire*, London, 1970

Fowden, G. *Qusayr 'Amra: Art and the Umayyad Elite in Late Antique Syria*, University of California Press, 2004

Glubb, Sir J. B. *The Story of the Arab Legion*, London 1946

Glubb, Sir J. B. *The Changing Scenes of Life: An Autobiography*, London 1983

Goodwin, J. *Lords of the Horizons: A History of the Ottoman Empire*, London, 1999

Groom, N. *Frankincense and Myrrh: A Study of the Arabian Incense Trade*, London and New York, 1981

Hammond, P.C. *The Nabateans, their history, culture, archaeology*, Studies in Mediterranean Archaeology, XXXVII, Sweden, 1973

Healey, J.F. *The Religion of the Nabateans. A Conspectus*, Leiden, 2001

Helms, S.W. *Jawa. Lost City of the Black Desert*, London, 1980

Herodotus, *The Histories*, Penguin, 1954

Horden, P. and Purcell, N. *The Corrupting Sea: A Study of Mediterranean History*, Blackwell, 2000.

Hourani, A. *A History of the Arab Peoples*, London, 1991

Josephus, *The Jewish War*, Penguin, 1981

Khouri, R. *The Antiquities of the Jordan Rift Valley*, Jordan, 1988

Kirkbride, A. S. *A Crackle of Thorns*, London 1956

Lankaster Harding, G. *The Antiquities of Jordan*, London 1990

Lawrence, T.E. *Seven Pillars of Wisdom*, London, 1935 ed.

Lewis, B. *The Middle East*, London, 1995

Lewis, B. *The Arabs in History*, Oxford, 1993

Lewis, B. *The Assassins*, London, 1967

Lewis, N. N. *Nomads and Settlers in Syria and Jordan, 1800-1980*, Cambridge, 1987

Lunt, J. *Hussein of Jordan: A Political Biography*, London 1989

Maalouf, A. *The Crusades through Arab Eyes*, London 1984

Markoe, G. (ed.) *Petra Rediscovered*, The Cincinnati Art Museum, 1999

McDonald, B., Adams, r. and Bienkowski P. (eds.) *The Archaeology of Jordan*, Sheffield, 2001

Norwich, J. J. *A Short History of Byzantium*, Penguin, 1997

Perowne, S. *The Life and Times of Herod the Great*, London, 1957, 2003.

Piccirillo, M. *The Mosaics of Jordan*, American Center of Oriental Research, 1993

Riley-Smith, J. *The Oxford History of the Crusades*, Oxford University Press, 2000

Robins, P. *A History of Jordan*, Cambridge University Press, 2004

Salibi, K. *The Modern History of Jordan*, I. B. Tauris, 1998

Shlaim, A. *Collusion Across Jordan: King Abdullah, the Zionist Movement and the Partition of Palestine*, Oxford, 1988

Shlaim, A. *War and Peace in the Middle East*, Penguin, 1994

The Holy Sites of Jordan, Turab, 1999

The Penguin Atlas of World History, Vol. 1, Penguin, 1974

Vine, P. *Jewels of the Kingdom: the Heritage of Jordan*, Immel, 1997

Weir, S. *The Bedouin*, British Museum, London, 1990

Wilson, M. *King Abdullah, Britain and the Making of Jordan*, Cambridge, 1987

Zayadine, F. *Caravan Routes between Egypt and Nabataea and the Voyage of Sultan Baibars to Petra in 1976*, Studies in the History and Archaeology of Jordan II, 1985 : 159-174.

Zayadine, F. *Petra and the Caravan Cities*, Amman, 1990

Photography credits

Acknowledgements

My thanks to H M Queen Rania Al Abdullah for writing the Foreword and to her staff, including Rania Attallah, Kathleen Riley, Ghalia Alul, Najla El Haque and Aline Banayan.

Ambassador Timoor Daghestani and Nader Tarawneh in London, the Jordanian Tourism Board and the Department of Antiquities in Amman are owed special mention. My particular thanks are due to Khaled Irani and his staff at the Royal Society for the Conservation of Nature (RSCN), who perform miracles in Jordan with such little resources.

Some books are born out of an odd mix of circumstance, coincidence and inspiration and this book owes a particular debt of gratitude to a host of Jordanian, and non-nationals with vision and dedication to their country, and to the subject. Margaret and Ihsan Shurdom have been helpful from the outset, along with Maha Khatib and Patricia Salti.

Rana Sabbagh Gargour guided me through the Jordanian polity, and like many other new friends along the way, ensured the success of the project. People like Jennifer Hammarneh, Lucie Aslou, Imad Fakhoury, Fadi Ghandour, Jane Taylor, Tony Sabbagh, Mohammed Attiyeh and others.

But the principal single contributor of local passion for the book is Ammar Khammash, a true Jordanian patriot and *Renaissance Man*, who acted as my spiritual guide for the entire journey, becoming a worthy companion photographer to the book along the way.

As for my own production and editorial team, I am deeply indebted to Christa Paula for her meticulous hard work in collating, coordinating and writing the book. To Roger Fawcett Tang for his arduous journey of design and re-design, while David Saunders produced the images that flowed from my words and transformed the country to colour. To Koji Kawai for his beautiful nature photography; to Caroline Campkin and CS Graphics for hard work and forbearance, and to the many others involved.

The publishers wish to extend their gratitude to David Symes, Royal Jordanian Airlines, Yassin Talhouni and Lina Annab of Zara Holdings, Zohrab, Franco Scurelli and Katrina Hamarneh of the Madaba Mosaic School, Omar Abu Eid, Brighter PR London, the Irbid Archaeological Museum, Edgar Solenthaler, Tamara Khalil, Kay Boardman, Basel Ahmad, Hussein Hamad, the Maan Folklore Music Band, Nofa Safer, Hala Lukasha, Nouha Khalifa, Ali Maher, Dr. Konstantinos Politis, Adrian Cross, Aussie Martin and last but not least, George Szamuely.

Hossein Amirsadeghi